"This welcome collaboration between two key scholars of environmental culture explains why embracing complexity, pluralism, difficulty, and uncertainty leads to better, deeper responses to environmental troubles. In clear prose with wide intellectual reference, Bauman and O'Brien argue that 'radical change is possible only at the pace of ambiguity.'"

Willis Jenkins, Professor of Religious Studies & Environmental Humanities at the University of Virginia, USA

"*Environmental Ethics and Uncertainty* is original, engaging, and important. It offers students and other readers an entry into some of the very complex and challenging moral and theoretical issues related to climate change in a way that is smart and well-grounded without being overly dry, dense, or inaccessible. It does so by focusing on exactly the themes we need to be discussing in regards to environmental ethics and climate change today: ambiguity, uncertainty, pluralism, and hope. The authors show how uncertainty is not only theoretically but also practically helpful, as they think through concrete ethical problems such as fracking and pipeline protests. Further, their use of eclectic sources and thinkers both shows the wide range of issues and ideas we need to address in thinking about climate change and invites conversation with readers outside the field."

Anna Peterson, Professor, Department of Religion, University of Florida, USA

"*Environmental Ethics and Uncertainty* offers a timely intervention in polarized debates surrounding issues like climate change or fracking, and who or what we should believe. Drawing on the wisdom of activists and thinkers ranging from Rachel Carson to Martin Luther King, Jr., the book underscores the value of questioning. Bauman and O'Brien show us that excessive certainty and willful ignorance—both prominent stances in modern American culture—fail to capture the complexity of knowledge and its relationship to moral action."

Professor Lisa Sideris, Department of Religious Studies, Indiana University, USA

ENVIRONMENTAL ETHICS AND UNCERTAINTY

This book offers a multidisciplinary environmental approach to ethics in response to the contemporary challenge of climate change caused by globalized economics and consumption. This book synthesizes the incredible complexity of the problem and the necessity of action in response, highlighting the unambiguous problem facing humanity in the 21st century, but arguing that it is essential to develop an ethics housed in ambiguity in response.

Environmental Ethics and Uncertainty is divided into theoretical and applied chapters, with the theoretical sections engaging in dialogue with scholars from a variety of disciplines, while the applied chapters offer insight from 20th century activists who demonstrate and/or illuminate the theory, including Martin Luther King, Rachel Carson, and Frank Lloyd Wright.

This book is written for scholars and students in the interdisciplinary field of environmental studies and the environmental humanities, and will appeal to courses in religion, philosophy, ethics, politics, and social theory.

Whitney A. Bauman is Associate Professor of Religious Studies at Florida International University, USA. His books include *Religion and Ecology: Developing a Planetary Ethic* (2014) and, with Kevin O'Brien and Richard Bohannon, *Grounding Religion: A Field Guide to the Study of Religion and Ecology, 2nd Revised Edition* (2018).

Kevin J. O'Brien is Professor of Religion and Dean of Humanities at Pacific Lutheran University, USA. His books include *The Violence of Climate Change: Lessons of Resistance from Nonviolent Activists* and, with Whitney Bauman and Richard Bohannon, *Inherited Land: The Changing Grounds of Religion and Ecology*.

ENVIRONMENTAL ETHICS AND UNCERTAINTY

Wrestling with Wicked Problems

Whitney A. Bauman and Kevin J. O'Brien

Routledge
Taylor & Francis Group

LONDON AND NEW YORK

First published 2020
by Routledge
2 Park Square, Milton Park, Abingdon, Oxon OX14 4RN

and by Routledge
52 Vanderbilt Avenue, New York, NY 10017

Routledge is an imprint of the Taylor & Francis Group, an informa business

British Library Cataloguing in Publication Data
A catalogue record for this book is available from the British Library

Library of Congress Cataloging-in-Publication Data
A catalog record has been requested for this book

ISBN: 978-0-367-25911-2 (hbk)
ISBN: 978-0-367-25914-3 (pbk)
ISBN: 978-0-429-29050-3 (ebk)

Typeset in Bembo
by Taylor & Francis Books

CONTENTS

MAPS

ACKNOWLEDGMENTS

This book about ambiguity went through an appropriately winding and unpredictable process into publication. We started this project a decade ago and we thank all of those who helped it along the way.

First and foremost thanks to Rick Bohannon, who helped to shape the basic ideas and structure of this book and co-authored two chapters. While Rick's move into a new field of study and teaching prevented him from being a co-author on the rest of the book, it led to new insights into spatial elements and gave him the skills to provide two incredibly helpful maps. We are so grateful for over a decade of work with and learning from Rick, and look forward to decades more ahead.

We also thank our many collegial interlocutors at the Association for Environmental Studies and Sciences; the International Society for the Study of Religion, Nature, and Culture; the Forum on Religion and Ecology; and the American Academy of Religion who helped us to refine our ideas and give us such rich conversation partners.

We are grateful, too, to our partners at Routledge, especially our editor Rebecca Brennan and Editorial Assistant Julia Pollacco. Thanks also to the other wise editors who talked with us about this project, especially Wendy Lochner.

Our writing grows out of our teaching, and so we thank the students who helped us to think through these ideas at Florida International University and at Pacific Lutheran University.

Last and most, we both depended heavily on our partners for support throughout the writing and editing of this book, and the troubling world events that made the book seem all the more important and all the more challenging. Thanks and love to Imran Khan and Mary O'Brien.

INTRODUCTION
The problem with knowing the answer

On June 18, 2015, Pope Francis's encyclical letter *Laudato Si': On Care for Our Common Home* was released to the public. The day before, based upon a leaked draft, evangelical Christian critic of the climate movement Calvin Beisner published an opinion piece arguing, in part, that "Pope Francis actually considers climate change at most a minor issue," citing the fact that climate change "is the focus of only 2 percent of the encyclical."[1]

Beisner did not acknowledge that the encyclical contains sentences like this one: "Climate change is a global problem with grave implications: environmental, social, economic, political and for the distribution of goods. It represents one of the principal challenges facing humanity in our day."[2] Nor did he acknowledge that climate change is the key example of environmental degradation in the background of most of the encyclical. In short, Beisner's interpretation of *Laudato Si'* was wrong. But this was not surprising, because Beisner's interpretation was consistent with the message he himself has spent years spreading about climate change: the scientific evidence is unclear, human influence on the climate is ambiguous, and efforts to prevent climatic change will harm the economy and therefore the poor.[3] Beisner's initial argument about the encyclical assumed that it agreed with him; he read it through the lens of his own assumptions.

Of course, Beisner was not the only one to selectively interpret the encyclical. His opponents in the environmental movement resoundingly celebrated *Laudato Si'*, urging political leaders and citizens to read it and act upon it. But they have paid little attention to aspects of the document that are incompatible with traditionally progressive politics, such as its insistence that "concern for the protection of the environment is also incompatible with the justification of abortion."[4]

Politically and theologically, the authors of this book are far more sympathetic to the environmentalists who ignore Pope Francis's point about abortion than to Beisner, who—at least in his pre-release response—ignored the Pope's fundamental argument and the vast majority of climate science. However, this book is about what Beisner and progressive environmentalists too often have in common: a desire to find a single, overarching narrative with which to answer all environmental questions. Opposing such certainty is the point of this book, a point inspired in part by Pope Francis's encyclical:

It can be said that many problems of today's world stem from the tendency, at times unconscious, to make the method and aims of science and technology an epistemological paradigm which shapes the lives of individuals and the workings of society. The effects of imposing this model on reality as a whole, human and social, are seen in the deterioration of the environment, but this is just one sign of a reductionism which affects every aspect of human and social life.[5]

Pope Francis, like many other religious and activist leaders from whom we will draw inspiration in this book, insists that reductionist, simple answers are dangerous. The world is more complicated than any model or idea of it that human beings can create. Ordering our understanding of reality in just one way—*any* one way—is dangerous.

The desire for certainty is a dangerous and pervasive aspect of contemporary environmental debate, and this book will argue that a more constructive environmental ethics can develop when it is based upon accepting the inevitable ambiguity of human action, embracing a slower pace of discussion and decision-making, and admitting the complexity inherent in local communities engaging planetary problems. We seek the confidence that environmental historian Paul Wapner finds in "knowing that we do not know everything, and nonetheless finding ways to live meaningfully on behalf of life."[6]

Twentieth century philosopher Hannah Arendt also shared this goal, which is one reason she was an opponent of all attempts to strictly control speech. She argued that the public sphere is enriched the more it is built collaboratively. She writes:

> We know from experience that no one can adequately grasp the objective world in its full reality all on his [sic] own, because the world always shows and reveals itself to him [sic] from only one perspective, which corresponds to his [sic] standpoint in the world and is determined by it. If someone wants to see and experience the world as it "really" is, he [sic] can do so only by understanding it as something that is shared by many people … Only in the freedom of our speaking with one another does the world, as that about which we speak, emerge in its objectivity and visibility from all sides.[7]

None of us knows enough about anything on our own. We need one another's voices and perspectives to get anywhere near the truth. Freedom requires conversation, which only happens when we are willing to learn from others.

A German Jew, Arendt learned about restrictions on free speech by watching the horrors of Nazi Germany. But she also stood up against other forms of totalitarianism, including post-war suggestions that capitalist economics should be the unquestioned "common" basis for all public discourse. She insisted, instead, that people must speak freely and broadly in order to create a genuinely public space. When economic gain—or anything else—becomes the primary goal of politics, all truths and values are subsumed to that goal.[8]

This book is an argument for the importance of pluralistic conversations, what we will later define as "planetary" contexts that embrace the uncertainty inherent in any question about how human beings ought to live together with one another and the rest of the natural world. Uncertainty in politics and ethics requires experiments with counter-nationalist and counter-exceptionalist narratives. It requires inherently ambiguous acts that resist a culture tempted towards the certainties of unquestioned patriotism and simplicity. Such a reorganization will demand that we take multiple human and non-human perspectives seriously as we begin to forge diverse foundations for future possibilities of flourishing.

The biggest problems facing humanity in the 21st century require an acceptance of wild uncertainty. Those who claim to know "the answer" to our toughest challenges are in fact contributing to myriad, diverse, and wicked problems by virtue of that very certainty. This book will focus particularly on the challenge of climate change and its roots in globalized economics and consumption. No single moral principle, sacred cow, or ideal of progress can match either the problems of climate change or the diverse human communities involved in them. The path forward for concerned people in the 21st century is more multifaceted, more tenuous, and more deliberate than most public discourse suggests. We need an ethics of uncertainty, moving at the pace of ambiguity.

Background and assumptions

The authors of this book consider themselves environmentalists. By this we mean three things: (1) we are unsatisfied with the predominant ways privileged human beings in industrial societies relate to the nonhuman world, (2) we are deeply concerned about the problems of climate change, species loss, toxic pollution, and the unjust distribution of environmental benefits and burdens, and (3) we are committed to actively changing human thought, behavior, and institutions in response to these problems. This common ground of concern for the present and future of the planetary community gives us the energy to endure uncertainties.

However, much of this book argues with other environmentalists, doing ethics by thinking critically about the moral stands that we take in support of the three positions just named. Our argument is that the environmental movement will be better the more it understands itself as a discourse of multiple, diverse voices, embracing and engaging ambiguities rather than finding single or straightforward answers. Not everything needs to fit into the Western environmental narrative, or any other narrative. There should be no simple environmental orthodoxy. All of life, including human beings, will be better served by polydoxy in our (re)tellings of what it means to be a human being among other human beings, social systems, and the endless diversities of the world beyond.

We learn our ambiguous approach to environmental issues in conversation with the environmental tradition, building on the work of others who have developed similar arguments.[9] We also develop our ideas in extended dialogue with three key

3

figures in the history of U.S. environmentalism: Rachel Carson and Marjory Stoneman Douglas in Chapter 2, and Frank Lloyd Wright in Chapter 6. While we do not claim that these thinkers would agree with our perspective, and while we disagree fairly strongly with some of Frank Lloyd Wright's ideas, we find tools in each of these environmental heroes that help to develop and demonstrate the importance of an ethics of ambiguity.

The authors of this book are trained in the study of religion and are particularly attentive to the practices and beliefs that help human communities make (and remake) meaning, interpret (and re-interpret) the world, and develop (and challenge) moralities.[10] This perspective informs our approach to environmental discourse, helping us to recognize cosmological and metaphysical assumptions, appeals to the sacred and profane, and the importance of communities united by ritual and spiritual truths. Thus, we read the environmentalists cited above with particular attention to their religious ideas, and in Chapter 4 we will add two additional figures to the discussion: Martin Luther King, Jr. and Malcolm X. Neither spent much time engaging what we today think of as environmentalism, but each sheds considerable light on the role of religion in moral and political debate and so has much to teach 21st century environmentalists.

Using these perspectives, we will argue that environmentalism requires the sense of meaning, the attention to ritual, and the deep moral traditions that come from religion.[11] However, we will also caution against any who find "the answer" to environmental problems in a religious or spiritual tradition or seek to dismiss diverse ways of thinking as "heresy." Christian ideals of stewardship, Buddhist critiques of consumerism, and neo-pagan animism are powerful tools for environmental thought. Jewish kosher laws, Hindu asceticism, and the deeply spiritual Council of All Beings are important practices that can nurture environmental action. But none of these offers a certain or complete path forward. Religions, new and old, are relevant and helpful, but they should not be used to simplify the deep challenges of the 21st century. Indeed, one of the reasons they are so important is that they offer resources to do just the opposite.

This book engages religious and other resources that resist certainty. We need to engage voices that are critical of what we know, such as the prophetic and the deconstructive. Many of the conceptual parts of this book will thus be derived from engagement with complicated and difficult texts, ideas from contemporary thinkers who label themselves as postmodern, poststructuralist, and postcolonial. We will try to use these "post" sources in as accessible a way as possible, resisting the temptation to be simplistically confusing in our argument against simplicity. Those who find theoretical arguments too wordy and theoretical are encouraged to focus on chapters 2, 4, 6, and 8, which aspire to practicality. Those who find such practicality dangerously simplistic are encouraged to focus on chapters 1, 3, 5, and 7, which outline our theory in the fullest detail.

The remainder of this introduction will more fully articulate the premise of our environmental "ethics of uncertainty." The book will then progress to three sections that combine abstract thought with concrete implications: Chapters 1 and 2

4

focused on activism and social change, Chapters 3 and 4 focused on ethics and progress, and Chapters 5 and 6 focused on nature and the sacred. Chapters 7 and 8 then offer theoretical and practical conclusions, reflecting on the implications of our argument for key questions and issues that emphasize the inherent uncertainty of environmental choices. The sixth and eighth chapters are co-authored by Dr. Richard Bohannon, a geographer and a fellow scholar of religion who brings important expertise in architecture, mapping, and social systems.

Our goal throughout this book is twofold: first to argue that there are no simple or straightforward answers, and second to shed light on the ambiguous but vitally important path ahead in an attempt to prevent the more destructive elements of the ethics and politics of certainty.

Four uncertainties in environmental ethics

This book aims to engage in critical moral dialogue with environmentalism. It assumes the valid goals and important insights of key environmental authors and texts, but suggests that genuine respect for them means raising the hardest questions we know in response to their ideas and their actions. By way of introducing this method, we here engage with four important environmental texts and raise a key uncertainty we believe is signaled—if at times through absence—within each.

Justice

Perhaps the most anticipated and celebrated environmental text of the 21st century thus far has been the papal encyclical mentioned above, *Laudato Si'*, in which the weight of Catholic Social Teaching is brought to bear on the challenge of climate change. Environmentalists were excited that Pope Francis, praised at the time as "the most popular person on the planet," attended to the issue, validating not only the science but also the moral importance of climate change and using both to question economic and cultural globalization.

The document is nuanced, but perhaps its most central point is an insistence that environmental and social issues cannot be separated, that human beings are called to work on the challenge of poverty alongside the challenge of climate change. Pope Francis writes, "We cannot adequately combat environmental degradation unless we attend to causes related to human and social degradation," and therefore "a true ecological approach *always* becomes a social approach; it must integrate questions of justice in debates on the environment, so as to hear *both the cry of the earth and the cry of the poor*."[12]

This attention to the connection between human beings and the nonhuman environment leads *Laudato Si'* to a series of important insights and arguments. It argues not only that industrialized peoples have a responsibility to help poorer nations and poorer peoples, but also that there is an "ecological debt" owed by those who have disproportionately caused climate change. The document notes that technological development reshapes not only the external world, but also the internal attitudes and moods of human beings, and therefore our capacities to relate to one another. *Laudato Si'* emphasizes that war and oppression exacerbate environmental problems, and calls for integrated solutions to human conflicts for the sake of all creatures. This attention to justice and to the human elements of environmental issues is vital.

However, while it is beyond controversy that environmentalists should take concerns of human justice seriously, many questions are raised when anyone attempts to concretely apply this idea. Consider the encyclical in light of the work of Indian theologian George Zachariah, who also emphasizes the inter-connection of justice and the environment. Zachariah argues that any ethic coming from a dominant structure will be inherently dominating, while "the poor in their collectivity is an epistemic community that creates oppositional knowledge." He therefore calls for "a grassroots earth ethics" that emerges from "the subaltern oppositional gaze" of the poor themselves.[13] Zachariah entitled his book *Alternatives Unincorporated* to emphasize that genuinely just and earth-centered solutions to environmental and social problems can only emerge from those outside the mainstream, uncorrupted by the market, corporate, and colonial interest of mainstream culture. He bases his argument on prophetic Christian theology, powerfully expressing the New Testament teaching that the first shall be last and the last first.

In some ways, Zachariah's perspective and Pope Francis's are similar. Both advocate special attention to the plight of the poor and call privileged peoples to solidarity with the oppressed. But their basic assumptions are fundamentally dif-ferent: Francis begins from the premise that an integrated response to poverty and climate change can come from the institutional church with all its privilege and power, while Zachariah emphasizes that knowledge must be subaltern and oppo-sitional to be trustworthy. They agree on the goal of justice, but Franics seeks to create it from above, Zachariah to find it among the grassroots.

Pope Francis emphasizes that all of humanity must face the challenge of climate change together, and the beginning of his encyclical emphasizes that he is not writing only to Catholics or even Christians, that "faced as we are with global environmental deterioration, I wish to address every person living on this planet."[14] Zachariah cautions against such universalization, against knowledge that comes from above or from "everywhere." This is a tension inherent in any environmental conversation, a tension that not even *Laudato Si'* resolves.[15]

Francis's appeal to the best of the Catholic Church is inspiring, but Zachariah's perspective reminds us that the same appeal to authority can be used by supporters of neo-liberal economics or other grand, global ideologies. Zachariah's more local and grassroots environmentalism is therefore promising, but of course such localism also runs the risk of playing into the hands of xenophobic, isolationistic, and insular poli-tics. Protectionist ideologies that try to keep others out can be dangerous, as can colonialist ideologies that seek to snap others into line.

Environmentalists must work to create a more just world as part of the work of preserving the ecosystems and nonhuman structures that support all life. But doing so will raise many questions, many uncertainties: Can those who benefit from unjust systems fully understand the flaws in those systems? Can inherited institutions that have propped up unjust structures in the past be trusted to oppose those structures today? Who is equipped to direct and inspire efforts for environmental justice and harmony, and who must take a back seat and allow others to lead? Uncertainties abound.

Interconnectedness

Decades before Pope Francis wrote his encyclical, scholars and activists in religious communities were arguing that environmental issues and social injustice raise spiritual questions and then drawing on the resources of theology to understand the nature of the problem and its solution. Highly influential along these lines has been the "Universe Story" developed by Passionist priest Thomas Berry and mathematical cosmologist Brian Swimme, an idea that is celebrated and advanced by many of the most important scholars in the field of religion and ecology. Berry and Swimme argue that humanity is called to move into an "ecozoic era," which they hope will be marked by a pervasive awareness that "the universe is a communion of subjects rather than a collection of objects... . Existence itself is derived from and sustained by this intimacy of each being with every other being of the universe."[16]

A central moral of this universe story is that everything is interconnected, most frequently captured by the scientific fact that human beings and every single other being on earth are made from the dust of stars. This has been a profoundly inspiring idea not only for scholars but also for artists and activists like the singer Joni Mitchell and the co-founder of Black Lives Matter Patrise Khan-Cullors.[17] The root idea is that human beings can only live well when we recognize and respect our fundamental connections to other people, to other creatures, to the earth, and even to the universe as a whole. We participate in every process of the cosmos; our planet and our neighbors feel the implications of every action we take. When we realize this, we are inspired to act responsibly, carefully, and justly. This vision of interconnectedness has been influential throughout the history of environmentalism, and it teaches crucial moral lessons.[18] Interconnectedness argues against the pernicious and dangerous assumption that any waste can be put "away," and it resists the thoughtless belief that the earth could be somehow unaffected by human actions.

But, of course, the idea of interconnectedness is also ambiguous. Consider the point made by ecological scientists Timothy Allen and Thomas Hoekstra, who agree that everything is interconnected, but note that, from a scientific perspective, this "is only true in an uninteresting way, for the whole reason for doing ecological research is to find which connections are stronger and more significant than others."[19] What these scientists say about observation is also true of morality—we can acknowledge that everything is connected, but we are not equipped to responsibly account for every connection. We must make choices. The universe story, in its name and its development by a cosmologist, emphasizes the connection between people and the entire cosmos. Is that the most important of the virtually infinite connections in life and existence?

Religious ethicist Lisa Sideris argues that it is not, because a single story for "the universe" is too monolithic, too singular. She worries about a narrative that places human beings primarily in relationship to the entire cosmos. A worldview of universal interconnectedness implies that our most important relationship is to the universe itself, which might distract us from the specific condition of our planet earth and the very specific places upon it that we inhabit as individuals and communities. The universe story runs the risk of encouraging "a mood of self-aggrandizement, a kind of cosmic smugness." Instead, Sideris argues, what is needed in our time of environmental degradation is not one story, but a broad range of stories humbly shared. "No one person, or even community of people, can provide a story for the rest of humanity, nor should they try."[20] We are stardust, but we are also water, soils, microorganisms, cultures, and traditions. Different people will tell stories that emphasize different truths at different times.

The fact that "we are all connected" might lead us to a more harmonious coexistence. But if enforced as an unquestioned Truth, could it also permit oppression, consumption, and abuse? Perhaps a better lesson to take from interconnectedness is that we are always inevitably speaking from only a partial view of the cosmos's complexity.

Yet again, uncertainties abound. The truth that everything is connected to everything else raises questions about which connections deserve attention and emphasis and which can be left unexplored. The tension between Sideris and those who advocate the Universe Story reveals a question about how to learn from interconnectedness. Should we emphasize a global, scientific and cosmic story that incorporates everything, or should we allow more diverse, distinct, and less organized narratives from many sources?

Urgency

Environmentalists regularly face the temptation to ignore uncertainties in order to instead emphasize the urgency of immediate action. Consider Paul and Anne Ehrlich, pioneers in the environmental community who insist that their expertise as population biologists has important lessons to teach about the human species. Because we are animals like all others, they argue, we have a carrying capacity within any particular habitat. By extension, it follows that there is a certain number of people the earth can support. In 1968, the Ehrlichs published *The Population Bomb*, which suggested that humanity had already exceeded the earth's capacity to support us, and that significant degradation of ecosystems and mass starvation were inevitable. The tone of the book was urgent: "We must rapidly bring the world population under control, reducing the growth rate to zero or making it negative."[21]

Since 1968, the Ehrlichs' argument has become increasingly nuanced—taking into account technological developments and the fact that human beings can choose to consume less, thereby changing the number of our species that the earth can support.[22] But the urgency remains, and in a 2008 book they point out that while famine and shortages may not have occurred on the scale they originally predicted, the 21st century world is in fact torn apart by wars over resources, a clear sign that our species has overstepped its boundaries.[23]

The Ehrlichs' urgency is understandable; there are signs of overconsumption across the world, and such overconsumption drives other species extinct while increasing conflicts between human communities. While there may not be a global famine, over seven million people die of hunger each year. Even more widespread and disastrous starvation and death is certainly possible if the technologies that we currently use to feed ourselves prove unsustainable and irreplaceable.

However reasonable such urgency may be, though, it has not always proven correct. In 1980, Paul Ehrlich famously made a bet with the economist Julian Simon, in which Ehrlich picked ten commodities that he was confident would grow more expensive as population pressures increased demand. He lost the bet, and Simon won with a prediction that new technologies and human ingenuity would drive those commodity prices down.[24] As Ehrlich has made clear, this does not mean that his basic premise was wrong—human beings are indeed consuming irreplaceable resources. But his concrete prediction was wrong, and the time scale at which he has predicted global catastrophe seems unreliable, as well.

Anyone who makes predictions runs the risk of losing credibility, and environmentalists have too often fallen into this trap. A credible environmental discourse must be open about the fact that the world is complicated and so no one can account for all variables well enough to predict the future. Population, pollution, species loss, and climate change are all real issues in need of urgent action, but that urgency can only be honestly and helpfully communicated when it is balanced with inevitable uncertainties about what the future will bring.

Concern over environmental degradation is productive when it leads to action. It is counterproductive when it leads to the kind of urgency that pushes other voices into silence. Study after study shows that the most reliable way to slow population growth is to eradicate poverty and educate women. So it is worth considering that urgent concern over population may be less helpful than steady work to help communities feed themselves and educate every person. The best argument against this would be the existence of tipping points that will lead to drastic shortages even if the global population stabilizes. But we cannot know with certainty where such tipping points might be.

So, more uncertainty. We can say, though, that complexity demands more than just the fast solutions created under conditions of urgency. Environmental action is urgently necessarily, but doing it well paradoxically requires us to resist urgency so that careful, multifactorial, and nuanced analysis is possible.

9

Wonder

Environmentalism is inspired not only by urgency by also by wonder at the marvels and the mysteries of the natural world. To be concerned about climate change is not only to worry about human beings suffering through droughts and flooding, but also polar bears left in shrinking habitats and old growth forests threatened by unprecedented fires. While "nature" is a complicated term that may be impossible to define, there is something deeply motivating about seeking to protect the world beyond human beings that is often called "nature."

One of the most moving contemporary writers about the nonhuman world is Annie Dillard, whose Pulitzer Prize-winning 1974 *Pilgrim at Tinker Creek* remains influential. The book chronicles a year Dillard spent in Virginia's Roanoke Valley and captures the ways a small creek inspired her to scientific research, personal discipline, and theological reflection. A key theme of the book is that nature is wilder than any human can properly understand: "my God what a world. There is no accounting for one second of it."[25]

Never romanticizing what she observes, Dillard is particularly amazed by the prevalence of death and waste. She is captivated by entomology, and tells stories of wounded spiders in her house, a giant water bug in the creek nearby, and parasitic lice on nearly every creature she examines. She reflects at one point on aphids, tiny flies that eat plants and reproduce by laying an enormous number of eggs, most of which die: "If an aphid lays a million eggs, several might survive. Now, my right hand, in all its human cunning, could not make one aphid in a thousand years. But these aphid eggs—which run less than a dime a dozen, which run absolutely free—can make aphids as effortless as the sea makes waves. Wonderful things, wasted." This is but one example of the Dillard's celebration of the world's wildness and prolificity. And she continually notices how uncomfortable these facts make her: "If we were to judge nature by its common sense or likelihood, we wouldn't believe the world existed.... If creation had been left up to me, I'm sure I wouldn't have had the imagination or courage to do more than shape a single, reasonably sized atom, smooth as a snowball, and let it go at that."[26]

Dillard's is not an explicitly environmentalist text, and she declines ever to tell her readers what to do about the state of the world. But she has nevertheless inspired many environmental activists with her deep commitment to paying attention to the world and her observation that nature is beyond human understanding. She also offers resources for environmentalists who seek to protect nature from humans, as when she dismisses a herd of cattle as "all bred beef: beef heart, beef hide, beef hocks. They are a human product like rayon. They're like a field of shoes.... You can't see through to their brains as you can with other animals; they have beef fat behind their eyes, beef stew."[27] The wildness of the world can be interrupted by human beings. When it is, something is lost.

Dillard's book suggests a very different kind of environmental action than those discussed above, because she does not really discuss human beings. Her attention is on the nonhuman world. This is interesting, and raises important questions: To what extent is it defensible to protect "wilderness" or "nature" as distinct from human beings in an interconnected world filled with social injustices? What does paying attention to the nonhuman world by isolating ourselves within it teach us, and what does it conceal? The boundary between humanity and the rest of the world is ambiguous and constantly shifting, what are we to make of it?

These questions must be combined with those made explicit in Dillard's book: How much sense can human beings possibly make of the wild world? What does it mean to live morally in a world that depends upon death and predation? How do we explain our place within this world? Uncertainties again.

Climate mitigation, climate adaptation, and climate engineering

In a complicated world, it is not hard to point out that decisions are hard, or that other people's arguments and activism are limited. Our intention in the previous section has not been to dismiss anyone. Much to the contrary, we hold Annie Dillard, Paul Ehrlich, Lisa Sideris, Thomas Berry, George Zachariah, and Pope Francis in esteem. We value their ideas, and so we have sought to take them seriously, as we will seek to do with the ideas of many other thinkers in the chapters that follow.

To take these thinkers seriously includes criticizing their ideas and using those critiques to sniff out the uncertainties that inevitably characterize any environmental action. We do this not as a merely intellectual exercise, but to point out that all environmental questions raise inherent uncertainties, making them what Chapter 1 will define as "wicked problems." We believe that this premise is crucially important for anyone working toward a better world in which human beings can live more harmoniously with one another and other creatures. The uncertainties of justice, interconnectedness, urgency, and wonder convince us that there are no easy answers. We do not know where we are going; we face multiple confusing and unpredictable paths into the future.

Of course, some people use the idea of uncertainty to dismiss anthropogenic climate change and support fantastical assumptions and goals. It is, theoretically, possible that the scientific consensus on climate change is wrong, that global average temperatures are not actually changing, or that human beings are not the primary cause. We admit that there is at least a tiny bit of uncertainty here. But this is not a very compelling uncertainty, because those who cast doubt do so without much attention to justice—they seek to protect the powerful rather than the powerless—, interconnectedness—they suggest that actions have few consequences rather than many—, urgency—they encourage people not to worry in a complex world—, or wonder—they suggest that the natural world's structures are simple, easily explained and protected. They may appeal to uncertainty, but they seem to do so in service of a simple idea: the climate is fine.

In other words, the analyses arguing that climate change is a hoax are done from a place of simplicity and certainty, seeking to continue existing systems. Such simplistic uncertainty does not need to be taken very seriously. The people propagating these arguments tend to gain politically and economically from them. When politics and economics are ends in themselves, certainties paint over the real communities in which people live, communities riddled with ambiguities, uncertainties, and multiplicities. Authentic uncertainty does not seek a single perspective, an easy answer.

A productively uncertain conversation about climate change considers not *whether* people should be concerned and act, but *how*. For instance, how should those who take climate change seriously balance mitigation, adaptation, and engineering?

The mitigation of climate change seeks to reduce the emissions of greenhouse gases. An individual might decide to ride a bike or become a vegetarian to mitigate the problem. A city might construct an alternative energy infrastructure or new forms of transportation. A nation might place a tax on carbon dioxide emissions. Mitigation seeks to reduce climate change.

Adaption, in contrast, accepts that some climate change is inevitable and proposes new structures for societies to survive in a changed world. A coastal community might build sea walls and levees. An NGO might increase resources to fight a disease like malaria that has an expanded range in a warming world. A nation might begin to incentivize new kinds of agriculture to ensure that citizens will have food sources as growing patterns change. Adaptation seeks to create resiliency against climate change.

Any reasonable response to climate change will involve both adaptation and mitigation, but the question of how to balance them remains difficult. Do you join a rally for a cap-and-trade system that would mitigate carbon emissions, or stay at the computer to continue researching how shrinking glaciers might impact future water supplies? Both are desirable, but in a world of limited time and resources, choices must be made.

A third option is engineering, proposals which would not directly adapt human communities but instead tinker with the natural systems of the climate themselves, reducing climate change without altering its causes. Proposals include creating artificial clouds to reflect more of the sun's light, planting massive new forests to sequester CO_2, or building new technologies that pull climate-changing gases from the air and store them underground. No such efforts are currently underway at a significant scale, and a variety of logistical, political, ethical, and religious questions are raised by the prospect. But many experts predict that engineering is an important piece of the human future in a world of climate change.[28]

Should engineering be validated alongside adaptation and mitigation? Does the very prospect of creating technologies that solve this problem tempt us not to take the problem seriously? Or would it be irresponsible to ignore these technologies in a world where people are already suffering and dying from a changing climate?

Knowing that we must seek justice, that everything is interconnected, that the problem is serious, and that nature is majestic does not resolve the question of which choice is more just. Burning fossil fuels to help climate refugees or to share information about the problems of climate change is a good thing to do, with costs and limitations. Foregoing all use of such materials because they are the root of such problems is also a good thing to do, with costs and limitations. Developing technologies that can intentionally reverse some of the unintentional damage to the climate could help people; it could also harm them. What chance should we take? What better respects our interconnectedness with the climate: adapting ourselves to the ways we have changed it, seeking to stop our careless impacts upon it, or developing technologies that reverse it? Can we feel wonder and amazement toward a world fundamentally remade by human action?

We will return to these difficult questions in our final chapter, but even there we will not offer a clear answer; we will find no certainty. This discussion of mitigation, adaptation, and engineering represents the uncertainty and the ambiguity of climate change. We must do something, and we will never know with certainty what that should be. We will never know exactly what the future ripple effects of any given choice might be. This requires an ethic of uncertainty, which can only be developed at the pace of ambiguity.

Uncertainty in tough political times

We write as United States citizens at a time when our nation's political system seems utterly incapable of even admitting, much less responding to, the problem of climate change. What's more, the political system shows little capacity to respond constructively to this problem even when our leaders pay lip service to the reality and urgency of climate change. We are disappointed in our government and deeply worried about its future and the future of our world.

Our insistence on unknowing and ambiguity may seem odd—if not downright dangerous—in a time where fake news and outright lies are helping to sway public opinion. We complete this book in the midst of Donald Trump's presidency, in a nation still adjusting to the ways its President uses confusion about and denial of basic facts—such as the reality of climate change—to energize voters and supporters. In this political context, there is a renewed focus on the responsibility and ethics of news organizations to report the "truth" and not spread false information. Of course, we advocate responsible journalism, and we believe that truth and falsehood are real ideas with real meaning. But truth and certainty are two different things, and it is important to stand up for truth while still arguing resolutely against certainty in ethics and politics. Our argument is that destructive forces in the world are served by appeals to certainty and challenged by ambiguity. Utter disregard for truth is caused, in our view, by too simplistic a view of the world.

We want to unambiguously denounce the current president and the political system that produced him. But despite these temptations, we remain convinced of our thesis; we remain committed to ambiguity and uncertainty not only despite but *because* our political situation seems so dire. In part, this means we remain open to the possibility that we are wrong. Perhaps those who claim that market-based solutions can solve environmental problems are right, and the lack of governmental action is a good thing. We are very skeptical, but it is possible that we are mistaken. Admitting this allows us to remain open to conversation with those who disagree. Those people should know about our skepticism, but they should also know we will listen to them.

More importantly, we believe that our political system's failure depends on people who seek certainty and clarity. President Trump repeatedly frames every issue in simplistic terms of "winners" and "losers." He was elected based on an idea that the United States had once been unquestionably "great" and could be so again. His most oft-repeated proposal has been the complexities of terrorism, poverty in Central America, and increasing global refugees will be simplistically improved by the construction of "a big, beautiful wall." In a culture more open to ambiguity, we believe, this man could never have been taken seriously, much less elected. In a culture that recognized complexities, we would instead have serious national discussions about the nuanced but urgent problem of climate change. So, our stand for uncertainty is for a world where skepticism, openness to criticism, and genuine questioning are more widely accepted and embraced. We seek a world where, to borrow a phrase from Malcolm X, everyone becomes "critics of each other," because "Whenever you can't stand criticism you can never grow.... I don't think that anyone should be above criticism."[29]

Our response to contemporary politics is dissent and opposition, and we believe that admitting some level of ambiguity and uncertainty in our position strengthens rather than weakens that stance. It may be more satisfying to protest with full-throated and unambiguous slogans, but we worry that such simplicity is part of what led our country to this troubled time. We seek a future with more protest, more diverse opinions, and less clarity.

Time will pass. We cannot possibly predict what will be happening in U.S. politics as you read these words, and we hope that many of you are reading from other nations with very different contexts even in our own time. But we predict that our core argument will remain relevant wherever and whenever you read this: the desire for certainty is dangerous, it tempts people to ignore or silence alternative voices and perspectives.

Notes

1 E. Calvin Beisner, "The Ironies of Pope Francis's Climate-Change Cure." *The Washington Times*, June 17 (2015).
2 Pope Francis, *Laudato Si'*, ¶25.
3 See especially the statement on climate change that Beisner helped to write and promote: Cornwall Alliance, "A Renewed Call to Truth, Prudence, and Protection of the Poor." (2009): Accessed February, 15, 2013. http://www.cornwallalliance.org/docs/a-renewed-call-to-truth-prudence-and-protection-of-the-poor.pdf.
4 Pope Francis, ¶120.
5 Pope Francis, ¶107.
6 Wapner, *Living Through the End of Nature*, 205.
7 Arendt, *The Promise of Politics*, 128.
8 This is, in a nutshell, the argument in Arendt's *The Human Condition*.

9 See especially Wapner; Nixon, *Slow Violence and the Environmentalism of the Poor*; and Vitek & Jackson, *The Virtues of Ignorance*.

10 For more on the ways we define religion, see Bauman, Bohannon, & O'Brien, *Grounding Religion*, Ch. 1.

11 Again, we do not claim to be the first making this argument. In the field of Religion and Ecology, we particularly see ourselves as in conversation with Jenkins, *The Future of Ethics*; Peterson, *Everyday Ethics and Social Change*; and Kearns & Keller, *Ecospirit*.

12 Francis, ¶48–49. Although it is not cited, Francis seems to be referencing noted ecotheologian Leonardo Boff's *Cry of the Earth, Cry of the Poor*.

13 Zachariah, *Alternatives Unincorporated*, 101.

14 Pope Francis, ¶3.

15 For a critique of the encyclical similar to the one we find in Zachariah, see Gebara, "Women's Suffering, Climate Injustice, God, and Pope Francis's Theology: Some Insights from Brazil" in Kim & Koster, *Planetary Solidarity*, 67–80.

16 Swimme & Berry, *The Universe Story*, 243.

17 "We are stardust" is the refrain to Joni Mitchell's influential countercultural 1970 anthem "Woodstock." It is also printed on the cover of and as the introduction to Patrisse Khan-Collurs' memoir, *When They Call You a Terrorist*.

18 Consider John Muir's famous statement: "When we try to pick out anything by itself, we find it hitched to everything else in the Universe" from *My First Summer in the Sierra*, 110.

19 Allen & Hoekstra, *Toward a Unified Ecology*, 284.

20 Sideris, *Consecrating Science*, 8 & 200.

21 Ehrlich, *Population Bomb*, 161.

22 Ehrlich & Ehrlich, *One with Nineveh*.

23 Ehrlich & Ehrlich, *Dominant Animal*, 352–354.

24 On this wager, see especially Sabin, *The Bet*.

25 Dillard, *Pilgrim at Tinker Creek*, 267.

26 Ibid., 177, 146.

27 Ibid., 6.

28 See especially British Royal Society, *Geoengineering the Climate*.

29 X & Perry, *Malcolm X: The Last Speeches*.

1

ETHICAL ACTION IN AN AMBIGUOUS WORLD

In a 2014 *Rolling Stone* article, Al Gore offered "new hope for the climate," citing a variety of technological innovations and political reforms pointing to a bright future. He writes:

> It is true that we have waited too long to avoid some serious damage to the planetary ecosystem – some of it, unfortunately, irreversible. Yet the truly catastrophic damages that have the potential for ending civilization as we know it can still – almost certainly – be avoided.... . There is surprising – even shocking – good news: Our ability to convert sunshine into usable energy has become much cheaper far more rapidly than anyone had predicted.... . By 2020 – as the scale of deployments grows and the costs continue to decline – more than 80 percent of the world's people will live in regions where solar will be competitive with electricity from other sources.

Gore's 2014 essay is the sort of call to action for which he has become well known in the 21st century. He urges U.S. and international leaders to take political steps to support technological development and international cooperation. His tone is overwhelmingly optimistic, and he concludes by urging "genuine and realistic hope that we are finally putting ourselves on a path to solve the climate crisis."[1]

In a different way, Stephen Hawking's posthumous book *Brief Answers to the Big Questions*, offers hope for humanity's future.[2] Unlike Gore, Hawking does not have a record of optimism, and has infamously suggested that we humans have somewhere between 100–500 years before we abandon the planet. From the planet's perspective, this is quite pessimistic. However, like Gore, Hawking has optimistic certainty in the human ability to save ourselves. In his case, he predicts technologies that can get us off the Earth to start colonies in space and/or on other planets. While Hawking is vague on the details of what will happen to other planetary creatures and the people who cannot afford to be sent into space, he is confident of humanity's future.

Both Gore and Hawking represent a type of hope that this book is an extended argument against. We learn from Ernst Bloch's *Principle of Hope* that what they are

16

describing is not really about the future, but a projection from the present and the past.[3] In other words, Gore's hope is that we now have what it takes to change the course of the future and stabilize our planet, his hope is that the future will not, in fact, be all that different from the world we already know. Hawking's hope is that the very scientific thinking that helped to create the technologies that changed the climate will save us from human-caused planetary destruction. This is not the hope needed in the face of the "wicked" and multi-generational problems posed by climate change and the expansion of a global, consumptive economic system. Instead, complex contemporary problems call for hope amidst the uncertainty of what the future might become. Productive hope surfaces when we admit that we cannot be certain, when we lack confidence that we can solve our problems. Living with this uncertainty, we argue, is more important for the planetary future now than ever.

Carolyn Merchant helps us to identify the environmental recovery narrative of progress and solutions that Gore and Hawking represent so well. According to this narrative: a) there was once a paradisiacal planet; b) something such as plow agriculture, the scientific revolution, or the Industrial Revolution led to a fall from that paradise; but c) environmental technologies and practices can restore or recreate the lost paradise.[4] If this narrative is not straightforwardly true—and Merchant convinces us that it is not—then it is dangerous. Any confident prediction of a solution to environmental challenges reflects the problematic and destructive thinking that created environmental challenges in the first place.

To those with answers to environmental problems, we seek to pose questions. To those who call for progress toward a sustainable or post-Earth future, we urge a cautionary examination of who is imagining that future and who is left out of it. To those who confidently predict expansions of human technology and agency, we urge a careful study of the violence done by previous expansions of human capacity. To those who seek global unification to solve our pressing problems, we urge a humble examination of human and ecological diversity.

Confidence in human mastery, creativity, and control have helped to create one of the phenomena that will define our planet for centuries to come: climate change. We can also find such confidence in the face of a second and related phenomena of our era: economic globalization. Increased pluralism, more rapid interactions between disparate parts of the world, and the continued spread of neo-liberal capitalism across the face of the planet were created by the confident spread of capitalist and colonialist ideas. As the destructiveness of these forces becomes clear, some seek to solve it with the same thinking that created it. Centrist political leaders in the northern hemisphere argue that neo-liberal capitalism works, but simply needs more social and environmental protections around it. Populist leaders argue for a "return" to a past of nationalist or regionalist isolation. Both these groups seek to continue some past phenomenon, unchanged, and confidently believe that it will solve the ills of globalization. This book is about challenging such projections of certainty.

Confident predictions and projections continue the Western Enlightenment ideal of control over the world, which tends to posit a divide between humans and nature and insists that certain humans have agency while the rest of the world is passive. This has proven false, as·our attempts to control the natural world led to enormous unintended consequences, now demonstrated in the changing climate. It has also proven socially destructive—people of European descent who articulated this ideal too often assumed that women, people of color, and indigenous people were more "natural" than white men, and so should be controlled by white men in colonial systems. This is wrong, it does not work, and it creates unimaginably complex problems.

If we begin, instead, with the assumption that matter is active and that all human communities are a part of the evolving planetary community, such control becomes impossible. With this understanding, "Matter is not, alas, a straightforwardly quantifiable element, entirely graspable through totalizing and totalized formulas, maintained in secret and solitude by techie-experts."[5] Matter is vibrant and alive.[6] These are not new ideas—many animistic and pantheistic historical traditions across the globe have understood nature to be alive (even within the monotheistic traditions of the Western world). It is possible to draw from these historical examples without merely projecting the past onto the future. If nature is alive and active, then humans must learn to live within the community of life as perhaps a "partner" with the rest of the planetary community or a "citizen" of the planetary community. This means learning from the past but also developing new ideas to determine how a world of over seven billion people can try for this goal, which is a new question. Wrestling with that question is the essential task of building a future beyond our present challenges, and that will require an acceptance of ambiguity and uncertainty.

This book is also about living through and thinking beyond what many call "the Anthropocene." This is a geological period that begins with settled agriculture, mercantile capitalism, the Industrial Revolution, or nuclear fusion, and it is marked by the fact that the largest geological force is that of the human (*anthropos*).[7] The coming of the Anthropocene means that there may be no more "nature" outside of human influence, that we have created a layer of human culture and thought that spreads over the face of the planet. Some transhumanists and futurists welcome this era as a step along the way toward getting beyond our flawed biological embodiment and/or getting beyond the confinements of the planet itself. Others decry it as the death of nature or the coming of an apocalyptic end to the planetary community. In both cases, the language of the Anthropocene is problematic because it suggests that all humans are equally responsible, which is not the case, and offers a new spin on a longstanding injustice.[8] Perhaps the fossil-fueled era, the capitolocene, or some other name might be more useful,[9] but whatever nomenclature we choose, we need to learn to think about what is new and what is familiar in the current planetary era.

We hope for a world in which people take climate change seriously, prosper without degrading the world around them, and form human communities that can coexist harmoniously with other people and other species. However, we understand these as long-term and ambiguous tasks, distinguishing us from the mainstream environmentalist optimism of Al Gore, or the technological optimism of Stephen Hawking. Environmentalism must reach toward goals beyond our current reach and beyond our current vision. When schooled by the traditions of religious and philosophical thinking that teach humble acceptance, those who seek to protect ecosystems and work for environmental justice can recognize the ambiguity of our actions and the vital importance of how much we do not know.

This chapter offers the philosophical and religious foundation for the book by identifying and defining three central concepts: the importance of attention to planetary abjects (rejected or discarded bodies), the power of religious technologies for unknowing, and the potentials of a pace of ambiguity.

The planetary abject: undoing identities

Any assumption that we can solve our environmental problems must first interrogate the assumed and implied "we," asking not only who is included and who is excluded, but also what is assumed about identity and agency. For this work there is no better starting place than Judith Butler, who reminds us that human selfhood is performative, contextual, and shifting rather than established. Identity is always performed with and through multiple others, both present and past.[10] These performative identities co-create habitual norms, and norms always lead to the "abjection" of someone and something, the leaving out of something that is determined to be not a part of the identity. There is no identity without abjection, and so all human selves are co-constructed through interactions with what they are not. In other words, we are defined in and through our differences.

Within this relational understanding of identity, any organism or "individual" must be understood as created through their/his/her/its interactions with multiple others. Historical, cultural, biological, and imaginative trajectories all help shape the becoming of a given subjectivity (human or non), but we subjects have some agency, some wiggle room to shift the future of the ways in which we might become. Agency (the ability to act), like identity, creates abjects (something is not done or ignored by what is acted upon). By acting, the actor casts out certain bits of identity or, in some cases, whole identities or possibilities. In any given moment, we become in a certain way rather than another and thus some possibilities and actualities are "abjected" in the process. These interactions produce the condition of *differance*: that which is differed and that which differs.[11] Butler's task of queering ethics and politics means embracing *differance*, accepting the fact that the too-often ignored abject (leftover, rejected, or denied) is inherently part of our identities, and that morality calls us to pay attention to the abjects we create and the abjects we have ignored.[12]

Ethics is therefore a process by which one continuously re-thinks one's becoming in light of the conditions and implications of the differed and abjected, and thus recognizes the co-constructed natures of one's identities, politics, and ethics. By this logic, the goals of technological progress or globalization—affirming preconceived universalities and commonalities between peoples and multiple earth others—inevitably lead to unethical results, or at best a toleration of difference. By contrast, an ethic that begins from ever-changing and ambiguous grounds, from a place of pluralism and multiperspectivalism, asks questions about the abject and the other and relies on the differences between all creatures and the limitations implied by those differences.

This type of multiperspectival environmentalism is developed in the helpful text *Prismatic Ecology.* [13] The authors in this collection think about environmentalism beyond the color "green," which is tied to ideas of "pristine" natures and places within nature that are not urban. In a sense, the "green" focus in environmental thought favors a privileged understanding of nature that sees it as separate from the cultural and urban, which are understood as inimical to wild places. There are, however, many other colors in nature: brown, red, black, etc. Red is found in the blood of humans and other animals, in rainbows, in sunsets. Brown is essential for life that decays or excretes to become other life. Black is the color of humus, which nurtures the growth of all that lives (including the *hum*us that is *hum*an), and the color of the sea's deep darkness. Multiple colors are necessary to incorporate the urban, the rural, and the wild into environmental thought. By focusing so much on "green" nature, environmentalists have unconsciously abjected much of the human and non-human world from our ethics. In the words of some black critical theorists, the color "green" might help to create common environmental grounds for some, but the undercommons below the ground is just as important. [14]

Judith Butler's ideas and those of prismatic ecology help to *queer* environmentalist goals. Queer here is not meant in any derogatory way, but as a way to suggest that life is much stranger, much more complex than our concepts and language can imagine. The power and the challenge of environmentalism from a queer perspective is that we must think about ethics and identity construction while swimming in a sea of ever-changing differences. Those who seek universal values or laws will be frustrated by this rhetoric—to construct ever-changing identities and embrace wild differences is a tiresomely inefficient way to develop common ground and common goals. But this is its strength. Universalities are too easily used to ignore differences in the name of making some sort of progress; the undercommons is too easily ignored or backgrounded. [15] What if the world, from the largest ends of the cosmos to the smallest quantum realities, does not come neatly packaged? What if it is in fact our attempts to neatly package it that exacerbates ecological and social violence?

In *Meeting the Universe Halfway*, physicist and philosopher Karen Barad extends Judith Butler's notion of performativity, "all the way down" to the quantum world. In so doing, she seeks to loose the concept of performativity from the boundaries of the human species, developing an understanding of the world she calls "agential realism." This idea extends agency, usually reserved for some individual human subjects, to all levels of reality. As Barad argues, "In an agential realist account, *apparatuses are specific material configurations, or rather, dynamic (re)configurings of the world through which bodies are intra-actively materialized*." [16] Bodies, subjectivities, and entities are created in and through relationships with human and more than human "others." Thus, the abjects against which selves are defined are not merely human, are not merely other selves, but include all creatures and all matter from the quantum and sub-quantum levels to the cosmological.

Along similar lines, political theorist Jane Bennett articulates a "Vibrant Matter Creed" that affirms the reality of the other-than-human abjects all around us:

> I believe in one matter-energy, the maker of things seen and unseen. I believe that this pluriverse is traversed by heterogeneities that are continually *doing things*. I believe it is wrong to deny vitality to nonhuman bodies, forces, and forms, and that a careful course of anthropomorphization can help reveal that vitality, even though it resists full translation and exceeds my comprehensive grasp. I believe that encounters with lively matter can chasten my fantasies of human mastery, highlight the common materiality of all that is, expose a wider distribution of agency, and reshape the self and its interests.[17]

At the heart of Bennet's creed is awareness that human beings are one species among many others on an evolving planet. This changes the very idea of agency. Simplistic, anthropocentric arguments assume that humans are the most important actors in the world and that our actions determine the reality in which we live. They assume that ordering the world around humans (and only certain humans at that) is simply the reality of things. Arguing against such perspectives, Bennett reminds us that "there was never a time when human agency was anything other than an interfolding network of humanity and nonhumanity."[18] Recognition of human subjects as "assemblages," as co-constructed, as actors in a network of multiple other actors, or as parts of larger "hyperobjects,"[19] confuses any simplistic notion about what it is to solve—or even to seek understanding of—an environmental challenge. If there is no singular simplistic self that acts upon the world, then there is no singular simple action we can take to resolve our challenges. There is no enduring distinction between humanity and the rest of the world, so there can be no simplistic human mastery of nature.

These ideas from Barad and Bennett extend Butler's awareness of abjection to a planetary level, encompassing the broad range of other creatures and focusing in on the diverse layers of selfhood within each aspect of the world. To attend to planetary abjection is to recognize that "we" (human subjects) are inevitably made up of diverse selves, inevitably and importantly related to those people and those creatures we have actively or passively excluded.

This means, first, that "we" are never the only agents in the world. As theorists Bennett, Barad, Gilles Deleuze, Felix Guattari, Bruno Latour, Timothy Morton, and many others would agree, whatever the "I" might be, it is made up of multiple actants (things that are acted upon and active) and there are multiple other types of actants outside of and beyond the "I": histories, organisms, metabolic processes, social-systems, languages, systems of knowledge, climates, electrical grids, cities, etc. There is no singular "humanity" that can attempt to control the world. When we begin to see our own ethical actions—as individuals and as a human community—in relationship to multiple other "actants," we recognize that there are always others—human and nonhuman—of whom we are unaware. Our ignorance always prevents us from acting on behalf of the abjects we have ignored. Aware of our limitations, we must work to expand our attention. This is the humility that characterizes planetarity, an antonym of globalization's consumptive expansion.

Responsibility is never simplistically individual, no matter how politically or judicially expedient individualistic ethics might be. As Barad notes, "We are responsible for the world within which we live, not because it is an arbitrary construction of our choosing, but because it is sedimented out of particular practices that we have a role in shaping."[20] We are one conglomeration of actants among many others. Planetary abjection is not only a statement about the nature of selfhood, it is also a call to moral attention. If the abject is always-already a part of our identities, human selves should work to attend to the abjections created by each of our uncertain actions. Moral life requires rejection of transcendent notions of progress that move in a linear fashion "away" from our messy co-constructed realities, re-orienting us instead toward an immanent notion of concern and care for the abject around us.[21]

Attention to the abject also calls for moral attention to process over progress. Every action will have good and bad consequences, and these will be good and bad for differently embodied subjects. The reality of ambiguity challenges the pace of progress, because progress always outstrips what Teresa Brennan identifies as the "reproductive capacities of the planet."[22] Attention to process pushes toward a pace of ambiguity, focusing us on the geography of how our actions co-create multiple earth bodies in the present.

Such a reconfiguring of agency and time is a challenge for any moral, legal, or economic system built upon the idea of ensouled individual subjects, enlightened reasonable thinkers, Lockean liberal subjects, or even universal human rights and dignity.[23] All of these depend upon universalizing definitions, certainties, and ideals of progress. All emphasize commonalities rather than differences, and thus are more likely to ignore abjections. All reach for a global unity rather than a planetary awareness of abjection and diversity. Such unity usually ignores the abjects it creates—the indigenous peoples left out of narratives of "progress," the queer folk excluded from narratives of "natural" behavior, the people of color who have been implicitly and explicitly excluded from definitions of "human," the other-than-human creatures ignored in discussions of "human rights," and the cultural particularities lost in discussions of universality.

Any moral system that seeks evolution towards universality is dangerous for two reasons. First, misplacing concreteness onto categories such as "humanity" excludes others dismissed as nonhuman or not-as-human, who become morally irrelevant. Second, such concrete identities risk devolution into identity politics. Responsibility to "all people" based on something that all people have in common can too easily become a responsibility to "my people," in which only those to whom I have felt connection are worthy of my regard. Ethics that is based on common ground (to the exclusion of the undercommons on which those commons depend) too quickly devolves into ethics in which we care only for those with whom we easily recognize commonality.

What is needed, then, are new ways of thinking about the self and responsibility that rely on neither fixed identities nor universal essences, but upon uncertainty, performativity, and interrelation. As emergent theorist Terrence Deacon notes, this means:

> I am not the same I. On the one hand, I have somehow lost the solidity that I once took for granted, me-the-physical-body is no longer so certain; and yet on the other hand my uncertainty about my place of meaning and value in the scheme of things seems more assured with the realization that I may be more like the hole at the wheel's hub than the rim of the wheel itself.[24]

To recognize the self as an empty space, a hole at the hub of the wheel, the darkness we see in the night's sky, is to define the self by what it is not, by what is absent. It is to take difference and abjection seriously, and therefore to base the responsibilities of the self on diversity rather than commonality. Such a loss of the "solid" self is frightening for those of us trained to rest on foundations, but we will argue below that this more ambiguous self has long been uplifted by many religious traditions.

Misplaced concreteness essentializes human identity as a single, skin-encapsulated ego moving through time and space.[25] As Deleuze and Guattari notice, misplaced concreteness mistakes virtual reality for the real. They understand the world in Heraclitian terms: always in flux and radically immanent. They suggest that what we experience as solid things, even solidity itself, is actually virtual; the real is the flux of things.[26] Mistaking the virtual for the real can cut us off from the flow of life. This mistake does violence to the multiple earth others that are constitutive of our own beings (becomings). This understanding of the self is much more in line with the Buddhist understanding of the relational self (or "no self"). The isolated self is, accordingly, an illusion that causes suffering. Such an abbreviated definition of an individual human—ignoring the extended sense of self and limiting attention to a manageable individual—fuels the dangerous pace of industrial and economic progress, sacrificing the complex truth about selfhood for something that is more efficient to regulate and control.

Dominant environmentalist rhetoric seeks to impose common grounds: the "green revolution" sought to universalize farming practices across the planet; the economic development of "green jobs" seeks to universalize capitalistic structures; the abstract ideal of "sustainability" seeks to universalize an ideal of human culture to be indefinitely sustained. All of these goals promise the possibility of a rapid progress toward an ideal, but in so doing they elide the dependencies and differences (the undercommons) upon which responsible action is based. Such elision skips over the hole, the absence at the center of the wheel, the things that are buried under common ground, the space of the abject. In making a rapid pace of "development" possible and desirable, these goals also quickly outstrip the regenerative capacities of the earth and its co-habitants while creating more and more abject "others."

Environmental problems demonstrate the imbalance of such progress. The "global mobiles"—those who have the material, economic, and political power to perpetuate the myth of individual sovereignty—over-consume at the expense of the "immobile locals"—those human and earth others whose capacity for movement and change is literally destroyed by the actions of the global mobiles.[27] In an ethical system of universals, this is too easily missed—when the lot of "humanity" is improving, it is easy to ignore those humans whose lives have not improved and those who do not agree with the standard by which things are believed to be improving. When the tide is rising, those of us in boats can too easily ignore those who are treading water or drowning. And in a world where ocean levels are rising, this lifeboat metaphor is going to become more and more terrifying.

Planetary abjection focuses not on what is shared but what differentiates, not on what is present but what is absent, not on what is known but what is unknown. The visible universe only makes up about 5% of what we know and the rest may be "dark matter" and "dark energy" about which we know virtually nothing. This calls for a focus on the dark, unknown, undercommons. It is important to consider and to nurture a setting in which planetary abjection can be accepted, and to create a cultural habitat for uncertainty. The abject, the unknown, and the uncertain are as much a part of an ecology of becoming as the colors green, red, black, and brown are a part of nature.

Technologies of unknowing in religious traditions

The argument outlined so far is that selfhood is constructed from diversity, and so environmental ethics must be based on multiplicity rather than common ground, planetarity rather than globalization, process rather than progress. Many who agree with that argument will be surprised that we now turn to the resources of religious traditions, because religion is often associated with the fundamentalist assertions of universality and the destructive forces of globalized progress. However, this chapter joins a long list of contemporary voices in raising up the polydox, rather than orthodox, character of religious traditions.[28]

We view religions as living in the sense that every community of believers or adherents re-interprets meaning-making practices in light of their time and their context, and we therefore find in religious traditions records of deliberate and diverse debates about moral challenges. Understood across time, religious traditions are never monolithic, but are always-already hybrid, co-defined by inter- and intrareligious differences. Just as the planetary abject challenges boundaries of individual identities, so too it challenges the boundaries that separate religious traditions from one another and from other communities and institutions. Religions express human cultures' evolving responses to the challenges they face, and so

24

cultures facing environmental challenges have good reason to consult them for what wisdom might be applicable.[29]

Certainty offers a simple answer, requiring no "leap" in knowing to bridge the epistemological gap between our human context and our knowledge of the world. Every long-lasting religious tradition includes multiple resources to question and critique such simplistic thinking, technologies that help adherents stop seeking certainty and accept ambiguity, allow space for deliberation of abjection rather than immediate and thoughtless action. Religions offer tools with which to deal with wicked problems.

Many such traditions could be discussed: the apophatic tradition of Christianity that emphasizes how much cannot be said about reality, the *anatman* of Buddhism that deconstructs any idea of the self as absolute or foundational, and the unknowability of the Tao. Here, we offer three other examples of such religious technology for unknowing: The concept of *neti-neti* in Hinduism, Trickster figures found in many indigenous traditions, and the idea of virtue ethics found in Abrahamic religions. Each is conceptually relevant for explicating the importance of focusing on planetary abjects and the pace of ambiguity.

Neti-neti is a Sanskrit term meaning, roughly, "not-this, not-that." In the Upanishadic tradition, the idea of *neti-neti* is roughly associated with the *via negativa*, an apophatic approach to understanding the Divine. It means that once you develop an idea of what Brahman, ultimate reality, is, you can be certain you have misunderstood it. Our concepts, though useful for understanding the world, never capture reality. Rather, in every conceptual "grasping" there is a remainder, an abjection that remains hidden, a *differance*. In the Vedic/Upanishadic context, *neti-neti* can also be explored in conversation with two concepts drawn from Jainism: *anekantavada*, or "non-absolutism" and *syadvada*, or "multi-perspectivalism." *Anekantavada* means that we can never reach an objective reality from our contextual, located positions. *Syadvada* captures the idea that there are many perspectives from which to know the world, none of which is exhaustive, and all of which tell us something about the reality in which we live. Incorporating these concepts in yoga and meditation helps practitioners to realize that certainty is an illusion and that reality cannot ever be fully known. In a mindset of *neti-neti*, even to say that reality cannot be known is a simplification of reality that cannot be fully true. This is a rich tradition that teaches ambiguity.

Another relevant religious concept is the figure of the trickster. As Lewis Hyde reminds us, the trickster's role across a diverse array of indigenous traditions is to make the world through destruction. The trickster breaks down the concepts and boundaries that are believed to define the world, and thereby fundamentally changes reality.[30] This figure blurs the boundaries between humans and animals, the living and the dead, self and other, male and female, and even right and wrong. Their embodiment is always already trans-, it queries/queers the boundaries between concepts and entities. Such a blurring forces adherents to realize that every perspective is limited, temporary, and uncertain. Tricksters constantly make us aware of the excluded remainders in our thinking.

Finally, the virtue tradition in Abrahamic faiths also emphasizes the limitations of human capacity and human action. Judaism, Christianity, and Islam share strong traditions of virtue ethics, partly rooted in the philosophy of Aristotle. This approach to ethics is about habit formation, and a key element of it is that it takes time. Virtues are slowly cultivated over years rather than chosen or discovered in a mere moment. To seek virtue requires process rather than progress, patience rather than urgency. Concepts such as justice or temperance or love are fuzzy and relational, and Abrahamic faiths have rich traditions of complexifying these virtues, noticing the tensions between them, and reminding practitioners that final achievement of a virtuous life is ultimately impossible. This reminder of human limitations and the apparent tension between moral goals is consonant with the ambiguity raised up in this chapter. Virtues are precisely not certain essences of identity or reality. They are political imaginings, experimentations with which ethical actors might help shape the future becoming of life.

Religious traditions are internally and externally diverse, and no broad generalization about "religion" should go untested or unchallenged. Yet we offer a generalization for consideration, open to critique: religion offers tools to accept, wrestle with, and act upon the world's ambiguities, teaching complexity and uncertainty. Virtue ethics, tricksters, and *neti-neti* all point in the same broad direction: the wise and moral life requires an acceptance of unknowing.

The pace of ambiguity

Learning from religious traditions, paying attention to the abjects created by every action, we suggest that environmentalism in the 21st century must avoid progress and urgency, and instead embrace a pace of ambiguity. In a world of increasing natural disasters where the public seeks simple answers, this proposal may seem idiotic. We take this as a strength.

In *Cosmopolitics*, Isabel Stengers celebrates the ideal of the idiot, emphasizing that idiocy creates possibilities closed off by expertise and certainty. She notes: "the idiot demands that we slow down, that we don't consider ourselves authorized to believe we possess the meaning of what we know."[31] The multiplicity that constitutes any given identity changes the nature of moral thought, which cannot be about seeking the right answer for all people, but must instead be "thinking which belongs to no one, in which no one is right."[32] For Stengers, ethics should not be a debate in which representatives struggle to articulate the desires of their respective constituencies, but a palaver, a meandering and pointless conversation. Such conversation would seem idiotic to those who have a clear goal and seek immediate progress towards it, as Stengers's embrace of the idiot anticipates.

The role of the moral actor is "above all to remove the anesthesia produced by the reference to progress or the general interest."[33] Such ambiguity in dialogue creates open spaces for the possibility of the abject to emerge into our visual, auditory, tactical, and contemplative senses. It is through such a process that a more "common" world, a world that begins to notice and incorporate undercommons, can take shape. "The common world must be free to emerge from the multiplicity of their disparate links, and the only reason for that emergence is the spokes that they constitute in one another's wheels."[34] Again we find here the metaphor of the wheel's center: one person's "empty" center is the abjected spoke of another's wheel. Actants are multiply centered and the attempt to move too soon toward certain actions denies the emergence of the possibility of a "common" world.

This teaches a vital lesson about time. The rim of a wheel moves quickly, and for a competitive cyclist or a captain of industry rushing to file quarterly earnings, quicker is always better. But the emptiness at the center of the wheel is different. It is in slower motion, if it can be said to be in motion at all. The ethics of the palaver, of idiocy, and of planetary abjection must embrace such an ambiguous pace.

If there is a single, clear direction in which "we" should all move, then it makes sense to get there as quickly as possible. However, if morality is defined by diversity and every "we" contains multiple selves with multiple allegiances and interests, then there is no clear singular direction. In that reality, responsible action is deliberate rather than rapid, it moves not at the pace of progress but the pace of ambiguity. Jumping too soon toward a common goal abjects multiple earth-bodies for the sake of a transcendent, smooth place of arrival. Jumping rapidly to conclusions is the pace of industry and progress, accepting the common wisdom that we must quickly build, develop, and engineer our lives differently in order to bring about the environmental revolution. This leads to business as usual, the kinds of production that have degraded the world. The pace of progress makes for surface solutions that do not address the deeper challenges of the pace of progress in daily life.

As we argued in the introduction, it is dangerous to call environmental problems urgent. Environmental problems are severe, destructive, and expanding. But it does not necessarily follow that they are urgent. Urgency requires immediate action, but to responsibly declare a situation urgent requires that there be a clear, immediate action to be taken. Urgency without the possibility of clearly delineated action is fear mongering. Seeing a child walk blithely toward a busy street is urgent because there is a clear response by which to prevent unnecessary tragedy. Suffering severe chest pains is an urgent problem because it suggests the need for immediate medical attention. Trying to figure out who we are as a planetary community and how we ought to live with multiple human and earth others on the planet is not urgent. This will only be addressed emergently, over centuries, as we learn to pay more attention to the multiple voices that make up our planetary existence.

When tinged with urgency, environmentalist discussion takes on the tone of constant fear about an impending apocalypse, and we would do well to take lessons from those who have lived through the end of the world, such as Africans taken by slavery, holocaust survivors, and Native Americans.[35] From them we can learn about the complexity and challenge of living through the end of the world, and about resiliency. Environmental problems are not so simple as avoiding apocalypse. We do not understand what is happening and we do not have a clear path of response. Some things are always ending, some apocalypses have already occurred. Those of us who have not yet learned how to live through the end need to humbly learn from those who have. Environmental problems are as broad as civilization, as wild as nature, as diverse as human selfhood. The lessons of *neti-neti*, of tricksters, and of virtue ethics are all relevant, and all remind us that we cannot fully grasp such realities. So, we suggest that environmentalists take a break from calling our problems urgent.

It is better to present problems like toxic pollution, species extinction, and climate change as wicked. The idea of a "wicked problem" was first suggested by Horst Rittel and Melvin Webber, scholars of urban design and planning in 1973. They distinguish between "tame" problems that "are definable and may have solutions that are findable" and "wicked" problems "that are ill-defined," and can never be solved. "At best, they are only re-solved—over and over again."[36] Rittel and Weber emphasized that urban planning in the late 20th century was full of wicked problems: when one is negotiating space and relationships for a diverse community struggling with unrest and inequity that must adapt to changing values and institutions, the challenges are ambiguous and there are never clear solutions. The complexity of urban life continues, and expanding complexities of globalization and climate change only add layers to the wickedness of problems faced by human communities in the 21st century.

Environmental problems are wicked problems because they cannot be clearly defined. For example, environmental justice advocates variously argue that the core problem is the production of toxic materials, the distribution of these materials, the process by which production and distribution are decided, or the lack of attention to all these issues in popular discourse. Environmental injustice is real, but it is ill-defined. And it is not a problem that has a solution: pollutants, toxic and radioactive materials, and environmental hazards exist, and would continue to do so even if we stopped producing new ones today. As long as human civilization endures, someone will be making choices about how to distribute the costs and benefits of toxic materials. Conflicts about these matters may be resolved, but the problem of their existence will never be solved. Continued challenges are inevitable.

There is no space to think together in urgency, and so wicked problems call for something other than urgency. Wicked problems require space to think, space for multiply-centered actants to consider the diverse ways in which we view the world's complexities.

Wicked problems cannot be contained by the Newtonian simplicity of linear and predictable causes and effects. They even exceed the either–or of Werner Heisenberg, who preserved the hope of a future answer to uncertainty and so continues to inspire quests for a "theory of everything" in physics. Wicked problems are instead comparable to Niels Bohr's understanding of quantum reality, asserting a basic uncertainty at the deepest level of reality.[37] Philosopher Mary Jane Rubenstein articulates what this reality means for epistemology and ontology, writing: "The shape, number, and character of the cosmos might well depend on the question we ask it."[38] In other words, wicked problems are indeterminate, and every step we take to measure and understand them reshapes not only our understanding but the problem itself.

Human beings inevitably make decisions that will have unknown ripple effects and choose against options that will have other unknown ripple effects. The pace of ambiguity suggests that it is vital to spend time thinking through some of these unknowns before deciding, before making an ethical-ontological cut.

Wicked problems do not allow for absolute expertise or objective knowledge, but instead require an acceptance of multiplicity and diverse perspectives. Certainty is out the window, and process is far more important than progress. Movement will not be linear, and it will not be quick.

Even in the contemporary academy—perhaps especially in the contemporary academy—scholars are expected to justify their work based on how it serves some clear goal, whether that is discovering new knowledge, advancing a university's reputation, creating thoughtful citizens, or saving the world through some sort of technology transfer. These may be valid goals, but when it is assumed that all scholarship must adhere to one of them, the academy falls victim to a simplistic narrative of progress. The push toward technological transfer in the sciences and the "publish or perish" mentality play into the pace of progress. Work is produced ever-more-rapidly, to be read by an ever-shrinking number of peers and students with ever-shrinking time to think.

In the 21st century, technologies are produced to go to market without necessarily thinking about how they will impact the relations among humans and between humans and the rest of the natural world. When facing wicked problems, academicians, engineers, and all others need slow and deliberate thinking, not urgent action. In other words, the globalized, space-time crunch of the 21st century exacerbated by what some call the "great acceleration" of production and consumption starting after WWII,[39] might be best responded to with less action, by undoing the thought-habits that guide our actions to re-create false promises of progress. The pace of the palaver, of ambiguous conversations and uncertain hopes, may stem the narrowing of ethical concern that turns all of life into "standing reserve," for the human species in the name of some notion of progress.[40]

How, then, are we to proceed? We don't know, and this means that the process must be slow. Human beings in a complex world of wicked problems need time: time to think, time to deliberate, time to figure out how our imaginings take shape in the world that we think of as real. Paying attention to the abject of any decision requires time. Learning humility from the world's religious traditions takes time.

Ethical discourse as a palaver rather than a debate allows discussants to consider hope-filled "lines of flight" rather than unquestioned certainties.[41] To have a conversation with no apparent end is to walk in the shoes of an other: an other experience, an other way of becoming with possibilities that you might not have been able to imagine, an other reality that could possibly become. Such deliberation is essential in the face of wicked problems and necessary if we live in an indeterminate world. Deliberation creates a habitat for such thinking, pushing toward hope and action that can accept unknowing and learn from abjection.

The pace of ambiguity is the habitat for an environmental ethics of unknowing. On the one hand, it is much messier than an ethic of certainty and foundational justifications. On the other hand, it enables a sincere hope to emerge in the face of planetary ills. Hope for progress has a quick urgency. Sincere hope will take... much... more... time.

Conclusion

The three concepts articulated in this chapter—planetary abjects, technologies of unknowing, and the pace of ambiguity—allow us to more fully articulate the argument with which the chapter began. Where Al Gore is "almost certain" that the human race can avoid "the truly catastrophic damages" of climate change, and Steven Hawking is certain that the only way to save humanity is to create the technologies that get us off of Terra, we shy away from any certainties that lump all of humanity into one category. Instead, we seek to direct attention to the planetary abjects left out of a catastrophic narrative such as this one. The violence of climate change and globalization, as Rob Nixon notes, cannot be "grasped" by one group in a time or place or even by multiple groups in times and places. They must be understood through histories, genealogies, and varieties of knowing the world in which we live.[42]

While Gore's and Hawking's hope is for technological, political, and economic innovations to resolve the challenge to civilization, we seek guidance in the ancient wisdom of religious traditions, which in all their diverse expressions offer reminders that human beings are limited, human knowledge is limited, and human power is limited. To respond adequately to the wicked problems of environmental degradation will require judicious use of religious technologies so that human actors remain aware of these limitations and find ways to think and act responsibly in light of them.

Finally, while Gore is hopeful that there are solutions to climate change and so urges his readers to get on board these efforts immediately, and while Hawking urges us to prepare to leave the planet, we understand climate change as a wicked problem lacking clear definition and therefore lacking a single solution. Gore and Hawking celebrate progress, but we seek deliberate and slow consideration of environmental questions at the pace of ambiguity.

Unknowing and ambiguity are at the empty hub of what it means to be human, to be alive. We suggest that unknowing and ambiguity should also be the center of environmental thought and environmental action. The next chapter will seek to expand this idea in a more practical dialogue with the work of two activists: Rachel Carson and Marjory Stoneman Douglas. The "sea" and the "everglades" are entities beyond human comprehension, and these women served those entities by speaking up when others mistakenly and hubristically tried to control the world. Stoneman Douglas and Carson offer a powerfully ambiguous approach to the unknowability of nature, approaching ecosystems as ultimately beyond human control and understanding. They accept and wrestle with the limits to humanity in dealings with the rest of the natural world, and so help to demonstrate the potential of unknowing and the pace of ambiguity.

Notes

1 Albert Gore, "The Turning Point: New Hope for the Climate." June 18 (2014): Accessed July 3, 2014. http://www.rollingstone.com/politics/news/the-turning-point-new-hope-for-the-climate-20140618.
2 Hawking, *Brief Answers to the Big Questions*.
3 Bloch, *Principle of Hope*.
4 Merchant, *Reinventing Eden*.
5 Allan Stoekl, "Chartreuse," in Cohen, ed., *Prismatic Ecology*, 140.
6 Bennett, *Vibrant Matter*.
7 A good introduction to the formation of this geological era is Ellis, *Anthropocene*.
8 For a good critique of the Anthropocene, see Sideris, *Consecrating Science*, 116–145.
9 Moore, *Anthropocene or Capitalocene?*
10 See, e.g., Butler, *Excitable Speech*.
11 See, e.g., Derrida, *Margins of Philosophy*.
12 As Anindita Balslev has argued, perhaps the most important question we can ask of any ethical or religious tradition is how that way of thinking deals with "the other." See Balslev, *On World Religions*.
13 Cohen, *Prismatic Ecology*.
14 Harney & Moten, *Undercommons*.
15 On "backgrounding" see Plumwood, *Environmental Culture*, 27.
16 Barad, *Meeting the Universe Halfway*, 169–170. Emphasis in original.
17 Bennett, *Vibrant Matter*, 122.
18 Ibid., 31.
19 On "assemblages," see Deleuze & Guattari, *A Thousand Plateaus*, 3–26, 310–350; on "actor-network" theory, see Latour, *Reassembling the Social*; on "hyperobjects" see Morton, *Hyperobjects*.
20 Barad, *Meeting the Universe Halfway*, 203.
21 Latour, "Thou Shalt Not Freeze-Frame or How Not to Misunderstand the Science and Religion Debate," 32–33.
22 Brennan, *Globalization and Its Terrors*, 22.
23 See, e.g., Bennett, *Technicians of Human Dignity*.
24 Deacon, *Incomplete Nature*, 539.
25 Whitehead, *Science and the Modern World*, 51–58.
26 Deleuze & Guattari, *A Thousand Plateaus*, 99–100, 110.
27 Bauman, *Globalization*.
28 See, e.g., Keller & Schneider, *Polydoxy*.
29 In part, this section of the chapter answers Anindita Baslev's call to understand how religious traditions deal with "the other" and otherness, with religious resources for acknowledging our embedded, ambiguous natures within a becoming world of planetary others. Balslev, *On World Religions*, 3–16.
30 Hyde, *Trickster Makes This World*.
31 Stengers, "The Cosmopolitical Proposal," 995.
32 Ibid., 1001.
33 Ibid., 1003.
34 Ibid., 999.
35 See especially Yusoff, *A Billion Black Anthropocenes or None*.
36 Rittel & Webber, "Dilemmas in a General Theory of Planning," 160.

37 See Barad, *Meeting the Universe Halfway*; and Stengers, *Cosmopolitics I*.
38 Rubenstein, *Worlds Without End*, 235.
39 McNeill & Engelke, *The Great Acceleration*.
40 Heidegger, *Question Concerning Technology and Other Essays*, 3–35.
41 Deleuze & Guattari, *A Thousand Plateaus*, 9, 114–147.
42 Nixon, *Slow Violence and the Environmentalism of the Poor*.

2

THE DEPTHS OF AMBIGUITY

Ethical pluralism and wonder in Marjory Stoneman Douglas and Rachel Carson

We have argued that the pace of progress creates a temptation to ignore the diversities and complexities of other human beings and the more-than-human world. But what might the alternative, an environmental ethics at the pace of ambiguity, look like? Fortunately, we have historical hints at such an ethic, as this chapter shows by identifying the constructive ambiguities in the works of Marjory Stoneman Douglas and Rachel Carson.

Marjory Stoneman Douglas, "the grand dame of the Everglades," was instrumental in developing the political will that eventually led to the formation of Everglades National Park. Rachel Carson was instrumental in building the case to ban DDT, a watershed moment in environmentalism. Given these accomplishments, one might think that these women must have spoken with the clarity that characterizes so much political and moral rhetoric. However, we will argue here that a strong current of uncertainty informed and defined the ways Douglas and Carson changed human ideas about the world around them.

Wicked problems and the blindspots of certainty

> For wicked problems, which resist professional solutions because they outstrip a society's scientific and ethical competencies, a problem-based ethic needs communities that can invent new cultural competencies.
>
> –Willis Jenkins[1]

The previous chapter introduced the idea that planetary problems are "wicked," beyond the reach of any single expert, outside the scope of any single analysis, and bigger than the authority of any single human community. Wicked problems arise out of the complex and chaotic interactions between flora and fauna, between humans, technologies, and nature, between earth, air, fire and water. As ethicist Willis Jenkins points out above, these are problems that cannot be simply managed by the tools available. They require communities to change, to adapt in response to— and to some extent learn to live with—new challenges.

As examples, consider all of the unforeseen consequences of the implementation of social and environmental "solutions" that have been introduced and promised to provide a clear path of progress toward a better world. The Green Revolution in agriculture, for example, was meant to end world hunger. It successfully increased food production, but then also contributed to economic poverty and ecological disasters in India, Africa, and South America.[2] As some "developing" countries began to accept loans from the Bretton Woods Institutions to industrialize and modernize agriculture, those farmers who could afford such modern technologies indeed saw increases in crop yields. But these increases drove the prices of crops down, leaving smaller farmers with less and less, and eventually leading many to sell to larger, more successful farms that depend more heavily on global supply-chains and fossil fuels. The Green Revolution has helped to feed billions, but it has also increased poverty and consumption.

In a similar story, nuclear energy was supposed to be the "clean" power of the future when it was first introduced. But those who advocated for it had no solution for the radioactive waste it produced, and they still do not. That waste has been disproportionately located near and in marginalized communities across the world. So, even as nuclear power plants have produced electricity with a relatively small climatic impact, their waste has contributed to environmental injustice. Agricultural and energy advances create good outcomes, but also bad outcomes. There are so many factors that contribute to each and every process that the complex systems created cannot be understood in any simplistic way.

If we want to address the so-called "great acceleration" of agricultural and energy production and consumption, we have to look at global politics, global economic inequities, environmental history, religious ideologies, and so on.[3] This is true of any wicked problem. Good intentions can go wrong due to the complexity of interconnected issues and the wildness of any given planetary moment. One person's "progress" or "development" is another person's, subject's, or entity's "regress" or "underdevelopment." Solutions always create ambiguous effects.

At the root of many appeals to managerial certainty and simplicity is an assumption that human social systems and the physical systems upon which they depend will behave according to predictable rules. Such classical mechanics has an important place; predictable rules still explain important things about the workings of the universe, serving a functional purpose in many realms of our lives. However, to project the certainty of classical mechanics onto the entire universe or onto the chaotic cultures created by human interaction is a gross instance of the misplaced concreteness discussed in the previous chapter. The challenge of climate change and the ancillary challenges of a global energy economy and globalizing economic structures are more like quantum than classical mechanics, they require humble awareness of limitation rather than confident assertions.

Misplaced concreteness leads to blindspots of certainty—that which does not fit into our projection of certainty tends to be ignored.[4] We do not see the realities that do not conform to the narrative we have constructed, or if we do we dismiss them as foreign, other, annoying and/or frightening. This enables people to

THE DEPTHS OF AMBIGUITY

confidently continue at the pace of progress while the wreckage of the abjected remainders builds up to haunt that certainty.[5] It becomes harder and harder to resist certainties, because we become habituated to them and ignore their costs.

While we have much to learn from religious technologies of unknowing, it is also important to acknowledge that religious communities can be prone to the blindspots of certainty. Unquestioned orthodoxies represent a belief that a system of rules and interpretive lenses that have worked for one person or one community will work for all, backgrounding the needs and ideas of all those outside the dominant community. As feminist critiques of patriarchal biblical interpretation make clear, assumptions that there are simplistically "true" versions of sacred texts or traditions always background someone's interests.[6]

Science, too, faces the temptation of oversimplification. Mary Jane Rubenstein, for instance, highlights the orthodoxy of the inflation theory of Big Bang cosmology and the resistance among scientists to entertain evidence outside of the reigning orthodox interpretation of the facts.[7] It is a common temptation to make meaning of the world and to assume that the meaning we have made fully explains reality. But the task of a vibrant tradition—a faith community or a scientific discipline—is to question and challenge such orthodoxies, to never allow assumptions to settle so long that practitioners begin to mistake provisional ideas for foundational certainties.[8]

We have suggested that one clear drive toward destructive certainty—one cause of backgrounding the wickedness of the problems facing humanity—is the pace of progress. Uncertainty and complexity slow things down, making easy certainties impossible.

It is important to be clear, however, that we are not advocating nor celebrating uncertainty for its own sake. Uncertainty can be used to support an unquestioned advocacy of fast-paced progress, in which case it serves a destructive purpose, as in the example of climate denial discussed in our introduction. Such use of uncertainty to support the status quo is the "precautionary principle" at its worst: if we are uncertain, we ought not change. Furthermore, uncertainty and ambiguity also create a space for language of "fake news" and "alternative facts" to seep into public discourse. This is a huge problem in dictatorial and populist politics around the globe. We argue, however, that "fake news" and "alternative facts" are much more an instance of imposing certainty: I don't need to listen to anyone else, any "experts", or any "other" in order to project this "fact" or idea as real. The type of knowledge we are advocating demands that we listen to and take account of multiple perspectives.

The misuse of these concepts must not lead us to dismiss all precaution, to ignore all uncertainty. Uncertainty can be more constructively used to slow human action, to question our impacts upon one another and the world rather than to support the contemporary pace of markets and technology.

The perennial danger of wicked problems and uncertainty is the idea that if we cannot solve a problem, we can only fail; if we cannot solve the problem of climate change, then all is lost. Perhaps. However, in *The Queer Art of Failure*, Jack Halberstam argues that failure is exactly what is needed in the face of a system that has so long promoted heteronormativity and simplistic binaries.[9]

Certainty and the pace of progress come from attempts to avoid failure. The acceptance of complexity and the pace of ambiguity, by contrast, suggests that failure is inevitable and can be constructive. Failure in the face of a destructive and monolithic system helps to derail unhealthy progress so that we might be able to live differently together as a planetary community.

In many ways, Marjory Stoneman Douglas and Rachel Carson thrived at the art of failure. As women in male-dominated landscapes, they failed to conform to sexist norms suggesting that women did not belong in public life and advocacy. They failed to defer to others' expertise and instead created their own ways of knowing and acting in the world. They failed to separate a spiritual sense about the nonhuman world from rigorous scientific analysis of that world's systems. These failures allowed a different reality to break through into their worlds, reshaping ours. They worked toward solutions to planetary problems at the pace of ambiguity without allowing the spaces of uncertainty to be filled with business as usual.

Carson and Douglas worked with messiness and uncertainty to make radical changes that are better seen as disruptions to previous ideas of progress than straightforward progress themselves. Marjory Stoneman Douglas's efforts to save the Everglades demonstrate a multiperspectival interconnectedness that refuses to separate the urban from the wild. Rachel Carson's advocacy and "sea ethic" reflect a wonder and religious naturalism that refuses to separate human feeling from careful study.

Of course, even our interpretations of these two women contain inherent ambiguities. For example, while we believe these environmental pioneers support our argument for ambiguity, we are aware that they sometimes appealed to certainties. As the previous chapter made clear, all action assumes some certainty, however imperfect and partial. The fact that these were women fighting for new perspectives in a patriarchal society meant that they often appealed to rhetorical certainty in order to be heard above the noise of the industries, aware of what their respective breakthroughs would mean for business. However, we will show that even when they used such rhetoric of certainty, Douglas and Carson left a space for ambiguity and unknowing that allowed them to see the world in new ways, changing how all who came after them might live within the larger planetary community.

Marjory Stoneman Douglas: multiperspectivalism in environmental ethics

Marjory Stoneman Douglas is a central figure in the history of Miami and the Everglades National Park. With a life spanning 108 years (1890–1998), she was born into the aftermath of the Industrial Revolution and she witnessed two world wars and the rise of nuclear threats, the environmental movement in the United States, and the fall of communism and rise of the post- world in which we now live. Though an environmental advocate with influence comparable to Rachel Carson, John Muir, and Aldo Leopold, she is far less well known. This chapter argues that Douglas's brand of regional environmentalism offers a counternarrative to traditional, male, middle- to upper-class American understandings of environmentalism, leaving more room for environmental justice and bioregionalism. In other words, Douglas offers what we would identify as an early example of a planetary ethic that is, above all, multiperspectival. Her life and her work sought to bridge the social and the ecological, urban and wild, peoples and nature, native and white. Such an ethic is helpful in an era of climate change, when advocacy for thoughtful local attention in the face of a globalizing world are vital.

Though a self-proclaimed agnostic, Marjory Stoneman Douglas came from a long line of Quakers and abolitionists, and she credited the religious activism of her family with inspiring her political awareness.[10] Her multiperspectival approach was also likely derived from her journalistic background: her father was the publisher of what would become the *Miami Herald* and she began writing for that paper at the age of 25. The landscape of South Florida also had a huge impact on Douglas. Jack Davis writes: "South Florida, in other words, is an ecological hybrid. Unlike the tropics, the region has wide tracts of pinelands, yet the majority of the Everglades' vascular plants, including the gumbo-limbo and West Indian mahogany, have tropical origins."[11] This vast natural diversity surely influenced Douglas's embrace of multiple perspectives throughout her life and work.

Douglas's first political action concerned women's suffrage, but as Miami grew and developers began to drain nearby wetlands, she expanded her advocacy into what became the cause of her life: establishing, protecting, and celebrating the Everglades. This included standing up against the destructiveness of Miami's early development and the dismissiveness with which developers treated the Miccosukee Indians and the land. She was deeply concerned with problems that we would today label environmental injustice.

Douglas's most famous piece of writing was the 1947 classic *Everglades: River of Grass*. This book is famously difficult to characterize; as Michael Branch notes, it is nonfiction "with the feel of a novel, and the charm of a chronological procession of short stories," that is simultaneously "epic literary environmental history" and "a work of blistering environmental advocacy."[12] *Everglades* held many views together: at some points it explained natural systems, at other points it analyzed the ways native peoples in southern Florida sustained themselves in harmony with their habitat, and at still other points it fiercely promoted the preservation and protection of the land. This reflects a multiperspectival environmental ethic, pragmatically welcoming rather than fearing pluralism.

Despite its breadth, Douglas's work is grounded in a deep sense of a particular place. It begins with the sentence "There are no other Everglades in the world." This sense of uniqueness grounded her in an ecosystem long before bioregionalism became a popular environmentalist ideal.[13] An immigrant to Florida from New England, she wrote, "All we need, really, is a change from near frigid to a tropical attitude of mind."[14] She really understood that to truly live in a place (or in multiple places), one must allow those places to change one's mind, ideas, and ways of thinking. In other words, she recognized that landscapes shape "inner-scapes," and vice versa. Well before the development of "ecopsychology," she was making connections between the inner lives of

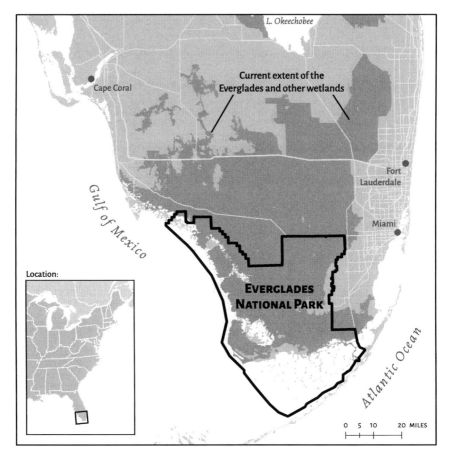

Map 2.1 The location of Everglades National Park in southern Florida
Sources: USGS, U.S. Census, U.S. National Park Service. Map by Richard Bohannon

human beings and the community of lives among whom all humans live. She thus contributed to the ongoing project of helping white residents of South Florida recognize the wonders of the region to which they had come, to learn to live more fully in place.

Douglas drew wisdom from the place itself, from its workings, from its vastness, from its people. For example, she critiqued proposals to drain the Everglades in order to farm them as short-sighted and laughably naïve:

> In all those years of talk and excitement about drainage, the only argument was a schoolboy's logic. The drainage of the Everglades would be a Great Thing. Americans did Great Things. Therefore Americans would drain the Everglades. Beyond that—to the intricate and subtle relation of soil, of fresh water and evaporation, and of

runoff and salt intrusion, and all the consequences of distributing the fine balance nature had set up in the past four thousand years—no one knew enough to look. They saw the Everglades no longer as a vast expanse of saw grass and water, but as a dream, a mirage of riches that many men would follow to their ruin.[15]

Such an appeal to the complexities of the nonhuman world as a cure against simplistic, unthoughtful "Great Things" is a clear example of the ambiguity we advocate. Douglas therefore offers an important contrast to much 21st century politics that emphasizes "dreams" and "mirages," instead insisting upon the complex uncertainties of the real world. Indeed, the fast pace of a fossil-fueled world encourages us to dream and think without any connection to the rest of the natural world. It literally lures us to live outside of the carrying capacity of the planet, at great peril for many humans and earth others.

Douglas herself remained profoundly aware of national and global issues and of the many ways in which her particular place was connected to the rest of the world. She powerfully said that "The Everglades is a test. If we pass it, we may get to keep the planet."[16] Her commitment to particularity was never provincial or limited; her entire life, Douglas remained open to the multiple voices and perspectives around her. She listened to the interests of natives, of developers, of government officials, and balanced all against the interests of the Everglades itself.

Douglas's openness to multiple perspectives meant that she found herself on different sides of environmental arguments: at times she sided with the Corps of Engineers as they sought to better engineer the "river of grass" in the Everglades. At other times she fought against Big Sugar, arguing that such large-scale agriculture could not coexist with the flora and fauna she loved. At still other times she spoke out against the use of plumage in 1920s/30s fashion, which decimated the avian population of Florida. She was polydox in her interpretation about what "ought to be done" in the Everglades, contextual rather than idealistic in her accounts of human–earth, urban–wild relations.

Douglas always weighed human and non-human interests and came out on the side that she thought would promote the most good for the entire community. This took lots of listening, observation and time. She offers a vital example of thinking and activism for the environmental movement, welcoming pluralism and moving at the pace of ambiguity rather than the pace of progress. This pace was dictated by the vastness of the everglades, a river of grass far bigger than any human can fully comprehend. She writes, "A man standing in the center of it, if he could get there, would be as lost in saw grass, as out of sight of anything but saw grass as a man drowning in the middle of Okeechobee—or the Atlantic Ocean, for that matter—would be out of sight of land."[17]

This comparison between the Everglades and the ocean suggests a link between the thinking of Douglas and that of Carson, as will become clear below. It also shows that Douglas treated her beloved river of grass as a place of mystery and depth. She could hear the multiple voices around her because they resonated and focused in one powerful place. This resonates with Keller's observation in *The Cloud of Unknowing*: "This could be the purpose of it all: an infinite conviviality tuned at every level and in every galaxy to its minimal participant and its maximum creativity, calling forth observantly ever fresh performances of relation."[18] Though Marjory Stoneman Douglas was no theologian, she had a profound ability to hear many voices in the communities around her, and she recognized the conviviality of those voices. This is only possible if one also recognizes the otherness of others—in other words, if one embraces unknowing. Standing amidst, with, and in the middle, one cannot take a certain, objective view of the whole; one must walk around and converse with others to get a better understanding. Furthermore, one must admit that we can never get outside of that locatedness to see any sort of whole, so we had better act accordingly. This perspective from within the Everglades, in the thick of things, might help us gain a "wicked" perspective to match the "wicked" problems we face today. Douglas's approach to the people and the creatures and the systems of the Everglades demonstrates an ethic of ambiguity at play.

Hers was not, however, a romanticized regionalism. She never lifted up some ideal of the surrounding ecosystem as a model of perfection separate from human affairs. As Jack Davis argues, "Nature and humans were not distinct [for Douglas], but part of one expansive, interconnected system. The urban environment, that of human species, was ecologically bound with the extra-urban environment, that of non-human species."[19] Understanding humans ecologically and seeing urban places as part of the natural world was part of Douglas's environmental ethic, distinguishing her from many other thinkers of her era.

Douglas's understanding of humans as a part of the natural world is an example of what Isabelle Stengers calls, "an ecology of practice."[20] Working with the philosophy of science, and more directly that of quantum physics, Stengers articulates an understanding of knowledge and value that is neither relative nor universal but contextual. Similar to Douglas's regionalism, such a contextual approach is necessarily ecological. It opens our knowledge onto evolving planetary communities rather than sealing us off into certain foundational and human truths. It helps us to understand how practices of various ways of thinking, being, and becoming emerge from certain contexts and return to shape those contexts. In this sense, even scientific ways of knowing have an "ecology of practices" that relate the scientists to other organisms and ideas, which then create certain types of knowledge. This is an acknowledgement of contextuality: even our own knowledge emerges from contexts and returns to affect those contexts. Thus, anything known is known within a particular "ecology" of knowledge.[21] This is not, as argued above, a surrender to "fake news" and "alternative facts." An ecology of knowledge, a contextual understanding of knowledge forces us to look to and learn from the many others (human and non) about the world around us, while "fake news" and "alternative facts" focus on promoting a single point of view regardless of context and regardless of others.

This contextual way of thinking is, again, represented in the way that Douglas critiqued managerial solutions to problems, refusing to simply impose a notion of "progress" or "development" onto the everglades. Douglas's ecology requires and implies an ecology of ethical responses. We do not suggest here that Douglas was a "post-" thinker like Stengers. However, her regionalism allowed an ongoing, evolving, and uncertain relationship between Miami, the Everglades and the peoples therein.[22]

In a culture that sought to silence native voices, Douglas heard these peoples and their interests, speaking out for them and for their right to speak. As Davis recounts:

> To her, the tragic drama of powerful people dominating both less pow-erful people and compliant nature ran like an unbroken thread throughout the history of Western civilization, with repeat performances played out in the Everglades. Her insights here prefigured the idea of environmental justice, which came to life comparatively late in the environmental century.[23]

Douglas resisted the received knowledge that western civilization had cultivated previously "empty" lands. Unlearning this, she instead listened to the many voices making up the unique histories and landscapes of South Florida. She challenged the caricatures of the Everglades as a dark and scary swamp that harbored runaway Seminoles, arguing instead that the native peoples had found a way to make a living and a culture in this living river of grass.[24] In a world that devalued the nonhuman, Douglas also listened to the grass and the eco-systems supporting it, and she gave voice to their needs. Her ability to hear plants, people, animals, and the connections between urban and "wild" enabled her to understand better the whole organism of South Florida in a unique way. She helped to ensure that the Everglades would not be drained, and instead become secured as a national treasure and ecological marvel.

Early feminist theologian Nelle Morton, a contemporary of Douglas, captures a similar attitude this way: "Hearing to speech is political. Hearing to speech is never one-sided. Once a person is heard to speech she becomes a hearing person."[25] Such deep listening is also important to the Quaker tradition in which Douglas had roots. She was, in fact, an exemplary model of "hearing voices into speech." A woman in science when that field was overwhelmingly dominated by men who challenged powerful economic interests, she had to face a great deal of criticism from those who policed the received scientific and political canon. By listening to the voices of the marginalized and the nonhuman, Douglas learned to speak up against the institutions around her, and not just those that threatened the Everglades. She understood that changing our ways of thinking to let human and earth others in meant that our societal structures would also shift.

Specifically, Douglas critiqued the structure of the nuclear family and the Victorian ideals that created it: "Many of society's ills grew out of dysfunctional relationships at home, she honestly claimed. Properly run orphanages provided a more salutary environment than some families she had known."[26] For Douglas, listening to the many voices meant also the possibility of living in what may be radically different ways so that those voices can be heard. The pressures of "family" were stifling for the type of work she thought needed to be done in the world, specifically the expectations placed upon her as a woman. Her ideas raise the possibility that "traditional" family ideals are part of the structure that maintain globalizing capitalism, part of the technology for isolating people into their own small islands of concern. Douglas's ecology of knowledge meant critiquing any such received wisdom.

Yet another piece to Douglas's unknowing and unlearning was her distrust of the government. Over the years, she grew more and more skeptical of "official" accounts as she began to see all the voices—human and other than human—that were left out and all the interests that were hidden within those accounts:

> Douglas routinely offered a flesh-and-blood example of how she had been a victim of undiscerning trust in government bureaucrats. Audiences heard an apologetic speaker say that when she wrote *River of Grass*, she had been beguiled by the miracle of equitable water distribution promised by the Army Corps of Engineers. "I thought then … that the engineers were going to fix everything …. I can see how wrong it was when they called it a flood control board." Describing her book's praise for the corps as "perfectly ghastly," she confessed that the engineers had made her a "terrible liar."[27]

Distrusting government, family, and authority led Douglas to question certainties. This meant that she knew far more than those with simple and straightforward answers. In other words, questioning knowledge-systems—official government accounts, the nuclear family, human–nature relations—created new possibilities for becoming. Douglas's gift was to seek knowledge from multiple perspectives, and to thereby recognize that she would never know everything. This pluralistic approach to environmental work is a model for the pace of ambiguity.

Rachel Carson: wonder, humility, and sea ethics

> Carson's sea ethic is perhaps most apparent not in what she wrote in *The Sea Around Us* but in what she chose to omit.[28]
> -Lisa Sideris and Kathleen Dean Moore

Douglas's relationship with the Everglades problematized any reductive understanding of environmental management or environmental ethics, blurring the boundaries between urban and wild and between humans and the rest of the natural world. Similarly, Rachel Carson's environmental writing provides vital examples for an ethic of ambiguity. While Carson is justifiably famous for *Silent Spring* and the lyrically scientific argument it made against the use of DDT, we will focus here instead on her moral approach to ocean life that Susan Power Bratton identifies as a "sea ethic" comparable to, and importantly distinct from, Aldo Leopold's more famous "land ethic."[29]

Though Carson at no point articulates a full-blown moral system, her relationship to and reflections on aquatic ecosystems have several components of what we would call the pace of ambiguity. Two that we will particularly highlight are her critique of human mastery and the importance of a sense of wonder, but first we will contextualize this ethic within her life and work.

Carson, an agnostic raised in a Presbyterian family, might anachronistically be called a religious naturalist. The mystery of the natural world provided the primary sense of value and purpose for her work. She was influenced by Albert Schweitzer's "reverence for life," and such reverence appears in the delicate balance she struck between objective scientific observations and respect for the mysteries of nature.[30]

Carson was brought up in an economically struggling family, and her education came at a great price financially and emotionally. But she was driven by her love for biology and for the endless wonders she found in the living natural world. Her research was not met with instant success in a sexist world that did not welcome female scientists. Perseverance helped her to get a job with the US Bureau of Fisheries, which became the Bureau of Fish and Wildlife during her time there.[31] Much of her work was devoted to sharing data with the public, writing stories about the science and conservation of important sites to bring popular attention to them. In her early forties, she became the chief editor of publications, but soon afterwards she left the bureau to become a full-time writer, a vocation in which she found success for the rest of her life.

It was as an independent researcher and writer that Carson focused her attention on pesticides. She devoted over a decade to researching their environmental and health impacts, eventually publishing what she had learned in *Silent Spring* in 1962. The idea that agricultural chemicals could drastically threaten ecosystems and human beings had never been widely considered, let alone accepted. This was the era of the Green Revolution, after all, and dominant rhetoric suggested that technology and science could save humanity from any flaw or lack in the natural world. As biographer Mark Lytle notes, Carson "quite self-consciously decided to write a book calling into question the paradigm of scientific progress that defined postwar American culture."[32]

Carson brought the same argument more subtly to her writings about the ocean. The idea that human beings could disrupt fisheries and ocean ecosystems was also uncommon and unpopular, but the "sea ethic" inherent in her writings offered an innovative and important critique of conventional wisdom. Working against the confident narrative of progress predominant in her time, Carson moved in the direction of unknowing, insisting on modest limitation of human action because of the undeniable limitations of human knowledge.

Carson's sea ethic entailed a great deal of resistance against the institutions of mechanistic science. She complexified the relationship between humans and nature, bringing something new to the previously patriarchal discourse of conservation and challenging the gendered idea that a masculine humanity could control a feminine planet. Though it is unfair to assume that Carson did or would have agreed with later ecofeminist critiques of masculinized science, she certainly challenged any simplistic and patriarchal assumption that human beings could master the nonhuman world. Sideris and Moore write:

> As Carson incorporated the human body into "ecology," she also began to resolve a longstanding tension between two distinct narrative voices with which she had experimented in her major works on the sea: the "heavily masculine" voice of the scientist who coolly organizes, interprets, and summarizes reams of information, and the more feminine voice of the "appreciative nature writer," the close observer and participant, expressing wonder and enchantment with nature's mysteries.[33]

Carson's work participates in what the last chapter referred to as queering environment discourse, destabilizing the ways views of nature are used to anchor gender norms. In doing so, she challenged both the "knowing" of established science and the "proper" male and female outlooks on the world. And, of course, she paid heavily for this: established science and agro-industry fought her arguments about chemicals by attacking her intellect and personal character in blatantly sexist ways.

The unknowing inherent in Carson's sea ethic was, in part, a question of perspective. She sought to understand the perspectives of sea organisms, imagining how coastal areas, shallow waters, and the deep ocean abyss would be perceived by those inside them. She emphasized that water was a non-native realm for human beings, providing a different—and far bigger—stage for life than that to which human beings are accustomed. Again, Sideris and Moore note, "Carson portrays the ocean as vast, indomitable, and omnipotent. Humans, by contrast are depicted as small and somewhat insignificant, as unable to control and master the ocean's power and to harness it for our own ends."[34]

Like Douglas, Rachel Carson understood what it means to think about the world from within rather than a god-like stance above it. Carson recognized that the rest of the planetary community needs its own space and is not something that can be reduced to the human realm. Learning from the limitations of human knowledge and experience, Carson sought to understand sea life on its own terms. Like Douglas, she hoped to "hear the many voices" into speech in her writing about the ocean.

In a typical statement that shows her ability to think about the ocean from its own perspective, Carson takes on the perspective of the sea floor:

> It is not the distance from the shore, but the depth, that marks the transition to the true sea; for wherever the gently sloping sea bottom feels the weight of a hundred fathoms of water above it, suddenly it begins to fall away in escarpments and steep palisades, descending abruptly from twilight into darkness.[35]

Here Carson offers scientific observation that inspires wonder and also assumes the limits of human knowing. This allows new insights to emerge "from the deep."[36] In yet another blurring of boundaries, Carson describes the life-cycle of mackerel this way:

> Of the millions of mackerel eggs drifting along…thousands went no farther than the first stages of the journey into life until they were seized and eaten by the comb jellies, to be speedily converted into the watery tissue of their foes and in this reincarnation to roam the sea, preying on their own kind.[37]

Here she captures the interconnected cycles of life, evocatively identifying with both mackerel eggs and their predators. Such descriptions decenter the human, suggesting in yet another powerful way the limitations of what people can know, what people can experience, and, by implication, what people can control. Carson's witness and her humility have transformed the world in ways that allow for many more planetary voices and connections to come to speech.

The depths and vastness of the ocean nurtured a sea ethic that apophatically emphasizes human limitations in order to lift up the wonders of the nonhuman world. Although Carson stopped practicing religion and made few explicit appeals to Christian ideas in her writings, Lisa Sideris argues that the Presbyterianism of her family influenced Carson throughout her life. Carson frequently appeals to a "natural instinct for reverence" compatible with Calvinist Christianity, and so Sideris sums up the resulting religious claim this way: "Carson simply asks us to reverse the telescope and discover our place in the amazing universe we actually inhabit, the world as it really is."[38] Carson's reverence for life included all human beings and all creatures, expressing itself in her work primarily as a wonder for the marvels and mysteries of the natural world.

Her sense of wonder at the natural world, informed by profound attention and analysis, also fueled Carson's moral positions. Her reverent wonder for the songs of birds, the health of oceans, and the thriving of human bodies drove her to publish, educating the public in hopes that they, too, would wonder at nature and thereby act more responsibly toward it. She was in no way certain that her struggle to bring more awareness to human–earth interconnections would come to fruition. But, like so many others who have changed the world, she hoped and dreamed for a different reality. In one essay, Carson wrote:

> Sometimes I lose sight of my goal, then again it flashes into view, filling me with a new determination to keep the vision splendid before my eyes. I may never come to a full realization of my dreams, but a man's [sic] reach must exceed his grasp, or what's a heaven for?[39]

In the end, Carson died of breast cancer, and many have suggested that her own disease is part of her life's proof that anthropogenic chemicals in the environment lead to unforeseen problems such as dangerous spikes in cancer rates.[40] Though there is no direct causality established between agro-chemicals and breast cancer, there are positive correlations. While those who desire certainty use the language of correlation to deny responsibility—there is no proof that humans cause climate change, or that industrial technologies cause cancer—such correlations deserve serious attention. Indeed, most of what we know is correlational rather than certain. To act only on "certainty" is impossible.

Since her death, Carson's legacy of wonder at the natural world and awareness of human limitations has only grown. Her sea ethic is a vital resource for the uncertainty of contemporary life. If human beings are limited and the world is vast and wonderful, it is advisable to slow our work, to stop in appreciation, to hear the many voices in the ocean, the skies, the land, and pluralistic humanity. This is the pace of ambiguity, which insists that we seek practices and policies in light of human ignorance, hoping not to simplistically solve but rather to adapt alongside the problems of our world.

Conclusion

This chapter ends by emphasizing a vital theme of the book as a whole: radical change is possible only at the pace of ambiguity; the pace of progress leaves room only for frenzied continuation of business as usual. Douglas and Carson offer extensive resources for radical change precisely because they offer extensive resources for slowing down to recognize complexity and ambiguity.

These two women also point to numerous other resources. Douglas attributed her earliest political activism to her Quaker grandparents. This points to a vital tradition that resists the pace of modernity. Traditional Quaker worship is conducted in a silent, non-hierarchical circle, waiting to be led by the Holy Spirit before speaking and listening openly to the leadings of others. Such space for silence, for truly hearing others and the ultimate, is a powerful form of resistance in the world that calls for constant action and progress. Consider Dalke and Dixon's analysis of Quaker pedagogy, which insists this tradition nurtures the capacity "(in Nelle Morton's memorable phrase), to 'hear beings into speech,' to invite the awakening of the unique narrative that constitutes the experiential insight of each person."[41] Informed by this capacity, Quakers have been leaders in advocacy for social and ecological justice and model a patience and open-mindedness that can be missing in other social movements.

Carson's sense of wonder can be traced in part to the ideas of Albert Schweitzer, whose deep "reverence for life" led him to leave the comfort and privilege of professorial life in Europe to become a doctor in what is now Gabon. This was motivated in part by a deep dissatisfaction with colonialism, and his service to African people was meant as repentance for the violence of his culture's previous treatment of the African continent. In 1931, when most Europeans still felt justified taking ownership of foreign lands and ruling their peoples, Schweitzer wrote:

What is the meaning of the simple fact that this and that people has died out, that others are dying out, and that the condition of others is getting worse as a result of their discovery by men who professed to be followers of Jesus? Who can describe the injustice and the cruelties that in the course of centuries they have suffered at the hands of Europeans? Who can measure the misery produced among them by the fiery drinks and the hideous diseases that we have taken to them? ... We and our civilisation are burdened, really, with a great debt... Anything we give them is not benevolence but atonement.[42]

Of course, a century later we must ask if Schweitzer's sense of debt had overly paternalistic undertones. But his ability to step outside the dominant progressive narrative of his society, to see the failings of his culture from the perspective of others, helped him to develop the philosophy of "reverence for life." This philosophy also reflected an ability to learn from non-Western cultures, as he traced the roots of his ideas to Vedic traditions that emphasize a relational understanding of the world.[43] This ability to start decolonizing the mind, to learn from many different peoples, cultures, places, and things without insisting that there is something inherently superior in western thought, is in dire need.

Many sources can help to build a way of life in the world that accepts ambiguity, embraces uncertainty, and acts cautiously while boldly resisting dominant structures. Marjory Stoneman Douglas and Rachel Carson help to demonstrate the powerful potential of ambiguity, multiplicity and connectivity to transform disparate hidden voices and bodies into action. Both spent a great deal of their careers and lives unlearning received traditions and "failing" in the eyes of dominant ideologies. This enabled new realities to seep into view, catalyzing new planetary voices that have since transformed the world.

Notes

1 Jenkins, *Future of Ethics*, 171.
2 For a good account of the problems associated with the "green revolution," see Ruether, *Integrating Ecofeminism, Globalization, and World Religions*, 1–44.
3 McNeill & Engelke, *The Great Acceleration*.
4 Plumwood, *Environmental Culture*.
5 On "hauntology," see Derrida, *Spectres of Marx*, 9–13.
6 See especially Trible's classic book, *Texts of Terror*. Of course, the scholars of religion who point out such limitations are also tempted towards our own orthodoxies, such as the longstanding assumption that religious traditions can be studied almost entirely through sacred texts, which backgrounded the practices and behaviors of religious people around the world who favored oral or ritual expressions to writing. See especially Hall, *Lived Religion in America*.
7 Rubenstein, *Worlds Without End*.
8 Kearns & Keller, "Introduction" in *Ecospirit*, 1–20.
9 Halberstam, *The Queer Art of Failure*.
10 Davis, *An Everglades Providence*.

11 Ibid., 28.
12 Branch, "Writing the Swamp," 127 & 132.
13 Douglas, *Everglades*, 5.
14 Frederickson & Davis, *Making Waves*, 59.
15 Douglas, *Everglades*, 286.
16 Quoted in Anderson & Edwards, *At Home on This Earth*, 179.
17 Douglas, *Everglades*, 12.
18 Keller, *Cloud of the Impossible*, 165.
19 Frederickson & Davis, *Making Waves*, 68.
20 Stengers, *Cosmopolitics I*, 207ff.
21 Stenmark, "An Ecology of Knowledge."
22 Bauman, "South Florida as Matrix for Developing a Planetary Ethic," 1–21.
23 Davis, *An Everglades Providence*, 35.
24 Ibid.
25 Morton, *The Journey is Home*, 206.
26 Davis, *An Everglades Providence*, 39.
27 Ibid., 497–498.
28 Sideris & Moore, *Rachel Carson*, 7.
29 Bratton, "Thinking Like a Mackerel" in Ibid., Ch 5. Chapters 6 and 7 of the same book continue developing the idea of a "sea" or "ocean ethic" in Rachel Carson's work.
30 Ibid.
31 Maguire, "Contested Icons: Rachel Carson and DDT," in Ibid., 197.
32 Lytle, *The Gentle Subversive*, 166–167.
33 Sideris & Moore, *Rachel Carson*, 8.
34 Ibid., 6.
35 Carson, *Under the Sea Wind*, 109.
36 Keller, *Face of the Deep*.
37 Carson, *Under the Sea Wind*, 75.
38 Sideris, "The Secular and Religious Sources of Rachel Carson's Sense of Wonder," in Sideris & Moore, 245.
39 Souder, *On a Farther Shore*, 30.
40 See especially Steingraber, *Living Downstream*.
41 Dalke & Dixon, *Minding the Light*, 13.
42 Schweitzer, *On the Edge of the Primeval Forest*, 115.
43 See, e.g., Schwietzer & Russel, *Indian Thought and Its Development*.

3

GOOD AND EVIL WITHOUT PROGRESS

Aldo Leopold's "The Land Ethic" is likely the most influential text in environmental ethics, developing an inspiring argument about the moral importance and practical necessity of land and ecosystems for human flourishing. Interestingly, though, his essay begins not with a pithy statement of its thesis, nor a stirring account of Leopold's own experiences in the natural world, but instead reference to a Greek epic: "When God-like Odysseus returned from the wars in Troy, he hanged all on one rope a dozen slave-girls of his household whom he suspected of misbehavior during his absence."[1]

Leopold wasn't merely showing off his Yale education. He recounts his understanding of Odysseus's extreme discipline to demonstrate a foundational concept for his essay: the extension of ethics. In ancient Greece, he explains, female slaves were considered property and their owner could treat them according to whim, without moral or legal judgment. Our ethics has expanded, and we now view such behavior as abhorrent. In the same way, Leopold suggests, we must learn to abhor the contemporary assumption that land is property and its owners can mistreat it without censure. Our ethics, he argues, must continue to expand, extending outward to encompass not merely all people but all environments. Such extension is, he argues, "an evolutionary possibility and an ecological necessity."[2]

Environmentalism since Leopold has contained few references to *The Odyssey*, but it has largely sustained his assumption that ethics is about progress and extension, that environmental degradation requires an evolutionary enlargement of moral consideration. Consider the highly influential work of Thomas Berry, who hopes for and predicts an ethical progress in which "human consciousness awakens to the grandeur and sacred quality of the Earth process", resulting in a global culture that exists in harmony with ecosystems.[3] A similar sentiment was expressed by Wangari Maathai in her 2004 Nobel Prize acceptance speech: "There comes a time when humanity is called to shift to a new level of consciousness, to reach a higher moral ground. A time when we have to shed our fear and give hope to each other. That time is now."[4] Moral progress is held out as a central hope in the environmental movement: as human beings develop the capacity to care for the land, for future generations, for the interconnectedness of life, we will learn to act wisely and sustain the world's ecosystems.

But progress is always based on a story, and this is dangerous if that story is simplistic or exclusive. Environmental geologist Lauret Savoy has powerfully noted that Leopold wrote as if the moral failure of slavery had been completely overcome in a nation that was still profoundly segregated, a nation that had forcefully interred its Japanese citizens just a few years before Leopold's essay was published.[5] Geographer Kathryn Yusoff makes a similar point, arguing that environmental origin stories tend to "function as identity politics that coheres around an exclusive notion of humanity (coded white)."[6] Leopold told a story about the expansion of ethics that drew on an idea of "Western history," neglecting both the ways that this expansion had not included all of humanity and the ways that any "progress" that occurs is never linear, never simple, and never irreversible. This should raise some cautions about any narrative of progress that assumes that expansion will always be inclusive, always be good. Progress toward anything is a movement away from something else.

This chapter and this book do not argue against progress per se. By definition, progress is a good thing: to be against it is to be against improvement, against things getting better. Aldo Leopold, Thomas Berry, and Wangari Maathai were profound thinkers and great activists who deserve to be carefully listened to. However, we will argue against the centrality of progress as a common goal. In 21st century discourse, we worry, progress has become an empty word that can and does mean many different things to many different peoples in many different contexts, and the challenges in contemporary environmentalisms highlight the dangers of a discussion focused on progress. The ideal of moral progress too easily creates a singular and urgent view of our problems, the solutions we seek, and the community that we make up.

Environmentalism in the early 21st century will be better served by a slower, more ambiguous set of diverse, overlapping aspirations and an awareness that movement toward any goal requires regress or stagnation in other directions. From a biological perspective, it is tempting to see the evolution of ever-more complex organisms as progress, but that notion must be tempered with awareness that the vast majority of organisms that have ever existed have been driven extinct by the same process. It is tempting to see the growth of industrial economies toward more production and technological development as progress, but vast numbers of non-human organisms and human communities have been degraded rather than uplifted by those changes. Any narrative of progress conceals trade-offs and regressions.

In what follows, we will develop two arguments against the dominant environmental narrative of moral progress: first, that it too easily assumes a single environmental problem to be solved; and, second, that it creates a sense of urgency pushing for immediate rather than thoughtful action. What is needed instead is an environmental ethics that steps back from the narrative of progress and works on multiple problems more slowly and cautiously. Progress is imposed over the face of the globe, smoothing over textural, embodied differences and flattening the world's possibilities for becoming. In contrast, planetary ambiguity ebbs, flows and meanders around the contours of diverse places; it hopes to create pathways toward which more planetary life might begin to flow.

Naming the problem: climate change as a network of environmental challenges

The word "environment" has been problematized by virtually everyone who writes about it, and few thoughtful writers believe that it is useful to speak of "the environment" as if such a singular entity exists. However, despite the fact that we largely agree there is nothing that can simplistically be identified as "the environment," many authors continue to write as though there is a singular problem with the environment, a "crisis" that can be understood as one category, one challenge.

In the study of religion, this idea can be traced to the field-shaping 1967 essay by historian Lynn White, Jr., who identified a singular root of "the ecologic crisis" in the anthropocentrism of Christianity, an anthropocentrism that he traced to the notion of "perpetual progress."[7] But many in the field of religion and ecology have used White's essay as a model for a different kind of progress, seeking a singular crisis with a single root.[8] For example, ethicist Michael Northcott spends a full chapter replying to White in his book, *The Environment and Christian Ethics*. He offers a nuanced defense that the Christian tradition should not be understood as anthropocentric, but does not challenge the idea that there is a single root to the problem. Instead, Northcott concludes that the core issue is "the money economy and industrialism," a force that "substitute[s] material wealth … for human community, ecological richness and local knowledge."[9] Industrialized societies have assumed that the market accurately measures progress and have abandoned the goal of sustainable coexistence with the earth. We have acquiesced to life defined by the market's selfishness and individualism.

Implicitly agreeing with White's assumption that there is a single problem with a single cause, Northcott argues that environmental degradation comes from capitalist modernity. This remains consistent in his more recent work on climate change, which traces that problem to what he calls "the original sin of capitalism": the reduction of everything, even the global atmosphere, into exchange value. So, Northcott critiques those who advocate the mitigation strategy of carbon trading and those who trust corporate technologies to re-engineer the climate. Such strategies are simply a continuation of the destructive marketization that caused the problem in the first place. The job of the 21st century Christian church, Northcott argues, is "to offer a theological critique of neo-liberal approaches to climate change" and to propose a radical alternative that takes the climate out of capitalism's control.[10]

Northcott's thought is too nuanced to embrace a simplistic moral narrative, and of course he heavily critiques those who assume that economic development and technological innovation represent unqualified progress.[11] However, by treating environmental degradation as a single problem with a single cause, he implies a sense of progress: we will heal the earth when we move beyond the excesses and blindness of capitalism. Northcott thus implies a clear path to a different kind of progress; his critique of capitalism's objectification of nature and of its tendency to separate human beings from our nonhuman context draws directly on upon Leopold's progressive land ethic.

Ecofeminist theologian Sallie McFague takes a similar position. Her views differ from Northcott's in many ways, but they have similar views on the cause of environmental problems. Like Northcott, she sees climate change as the most severe expression of a singular crisis facing "all people, all areas of expertise, and all religions."[12] Like Northcott, she suggests that the root of this problem is capitalism, which values only one thing: "the satisfaction of the desires of individuals through the means of constant growth." Market capitalism individualistically separates humans from one another and the earth, reducing everything to the status of resources. This global force is particularly dangerous because it has convinced so many people that it is the *only* option, that it is natural and inevitable. For McFague, this calls for theological critique: capitalism must be understood as "one of the most successful religions" in history, a religion that presents consumerism as the only path to salvation. She calls on her readers to oppose this destructive religion with a better one. She writes: "Christians, in our time, should see market capitalism as presently practiced as one of the most explicit and recognizable forms of sin."[13]

The dominance of capitalism is indeed a serious problem, and we agree with McFague and Northcott that economic philosophy and market systems serve as a global religion justifying and encouraging the behaviors that change the climate for too many people in the industrialized world. Economic gain as an ultimate goal promotes the kind of single-minded certainty we are critiquing here. However, we argue that it is a step too far to then suggest that capitalism is *the* problem. Climate change, like all wicked problems, is more multitudinous and complicated than that. If we switched to socialism, or any other economic system, at least some environmental problems would remain.

Consider the same move from the other side of the argument. Those who argue that the tools of global capitalism can solve climate change also identify a single problem and hope for a progressive world in which that one problem is solved. Bjørn Lomborg became famous in 2001 when he published *The Skeptical Environmentalist*, which uses statistical methods to argue that environmental problems are not nearly as bad as most activists suggest. Narratives of gloom and doom are useless, he argues; the truth is found in data: "global figures summarize *all* the good stories and *all* the ugly ones, allowing us to evaluate how serious the overall situation is." For Lomborg, these figures reveal that the world's situation is improving: "We are actually leaving the world a better place than when we got it and this is the really fantastic point about the real state of the world: that mankind's lot has vastly improved in every significant measurable field and that it is likely to continue to do so."[14]

Seven years later, Lomborg focused his method on climate in a book provocatively entitled *Cool It*, arguing that the solutions will come from the economic growth ensured by capitalism. The problem, for Lomborg, is the blind, panicked restriction on technologies that can ensure human development. The solution is to ensure that economic growth continues, such that future generations are wealthy enough to deal with the problems of a changing climate.[15]

Lomborg's arguments in favor of technological development and economic growth assume a narrative of progress that is too simplistic, overconfidently accepting that statistical analyses can predict the complexities of cultural and atmospheric change. This leads him to an overly sanguine solution: as long as future people are wealthy enough, they can solve their own problems. Lomborg has assumed that climate change is a problem for the future, not the present, and that people in the future will be able to deal with it if they are rich enough to invent the necessary technologies. He focuses singularly on one problem—economic poverty—and so develops a singular solution.

Ruth DeFries, a McArthur Genius fellow and professor of sustainable development, makes a related but more nuanced argument that also relies on progress to assuage fears about climate change. In *The Big Ratchet: How Humanity Thrives in the Face of Natural Crisis*, she suggests that history can be understood as a series of crises overcome by technological innovation.[16] However, each innovation leads to new crises. She argues that the current crisis of climate change is no different, and so predicts that human ingenuity will therefore offer a way through this crisis. Though we are sympathetic with this attempt to navigate away from simplistic views of technology and human history, we worry that DeFries's argument nevertheless still depends on a simplistic narrative of human progress. The story of continuously "ratcheting up" what we can get from nature in every crisis is a story of progress, assuming that there is a single problem—insufficient resources—to be solved with a single tool—technological development. Furthermore, DeFries's book, like Lomborg's, pays little attention to the question of who benefits from such triumphs and who suffers from the problems they create.

All four of these authors demonstrate the perils of identifying a singular problem and working toward a singular solution. Whether capitalism is viewed as a panacea to the world's problems or their ultimate root, singular focus upon it is problematic. Whether technology led us to degrade the environment or offers the path away from such degradation, a narrative that focuses exclusively on technology is dangerous. Both contribute to a linear view of the world: one problem can be solved by one solution. Environmentalists should not focus on the singular question of whether or not growth and innovation are the answer; environmentalists should not seek a master-narrative for global civilization as either the welcome embrace or the pernicious creeping of an economic system. We should instead ask many questions about the costs and benefits of particular economic and technological developments and the different impacts any action will have on diverse human and nonhuman communities.

53

Charging towards the solution: climate change without certainty

Predominant discourses about climate change have not only focused on a singular root to the problem, but also tended to urgently call for action in a single direction. This tends to be justified by the urgency of the problem. The logic is clear: If climate change is threatening the world in immediate and serious ways, then immediate and serious action is called for.

For example, in *An Inconvenient Truth*, Al Gore compares those who deny the threat of global warming to those who denied the threat of Nazi Germany and Imperial Japan leading up to World War II.[17] Two years later, Baroness Barbara Young, then chief executive of the United Kingdom's Environmental Agency, extended the militaristic rhetoric, boldly asserting that climate change "is World War Three—this is the biggest challenge to face the globe for many, many years. We need the sorts of concerted, fast, integrated and above all huge efforts that went into many actions at times of war."[18] In 2018, public intellectual Bruno Latour similarly referred to global climate change as "a situation of war," more dangerous than most precisely because the wealthy and privileged were ignoring it and pretending it was not real.[19] The message of such metaphors is clear: climate change is as urgent as the existential threat of war, and so requires immediate, unified action.

The premise is compelling, because climate change is threatening the homes and livelihood of many coastal peoples, it is changing the shape of the known world and the chemistry of the oceans, and it has already altered the stability of weather patterns that had been taken for granted for the entirety of human civilizations. However, this urgency does not create clarity on what should be done about it, and an emphasis on urgency alone tends to elide that fact. For example: Gore and Young appeal to metaphors about climate change that emphasize the need for *political* action. If climate change is like World War II or World War III, then what we desperately need are international and national governance structures.[20] They urgently push toward global political action.

A different scale of action might be called for if one sees climate change as a sign that global politics has failed and that the human attempt to live on a global scale is a failure. Wendell Berry is frequently lifted up as a wise sage for this perspective because he has spent 50 years arguing that environmentalism should stand in opposition to global and national answers. He argues: "Thinking Big has led us to the two biggest and cheapest political dodges of our time: plan-making and law-making." By contrast, "the citizen who is willing to Think Little, and, accepting the discipline of that, to go ahead on his own, is already solving the problem."[21] While Berry does not focus his writing or activism directly on climate change, he critiques industrialized, nationalized, and universalizing activities precisely because they have "accepted universal pollution and global warming as normal costs of doing business."[22]

The right response to a problem like climate change, Berry suggests, is investment in and commitment to local communities, as opposed to the kinds of coordinated national and international action that led to the problem in the first place.

This thinking inspires activists like Colin Beavan, who named himself "No Impact Man" while spending a year working to eliminate his carbon footprint entirely. Feeling helpless to make any change in global responses to climate change, he focused instead on what he could control: his own life. "I was coming to think my political views had too often been about changing other people," he writes. "I made the mistake of thinking that condemning other people's misdeeds somehow made me virtuous." Instead of preaching to and about others, he decided, "Maybe I ought first to worry about changing myself."[23]

The ethics developed in this book does not advocate the local over the global solution, nor vice versa. Rather, our work is more modest, observing that the reasonableness of both arguments suggests that there will be no single clear answer to climate change. Faced with a changing climate, should the world come together to invent new solutions, or should diverse communities stop trying to live at a global scale and instead commit to local answers for local problems? This is just one question facing climate activists, who must also balance mitigation and adaptation, threatened human communities and threatened ecosystems, contemporary challenges with future catastrophes.

Climate change is immediate, but we do not know what to do about it because we cannot make it just one kind of problem. It is global and local, it is revolutionary and evolutionary, it is social and environmental, it is present and future. Given this diversity of diagnoses and prescriptions, urgency is a luxury we cannot afford. The answer to diverse views is not to argue until we all agree on one explanation for climate change, but instead to accept that we face a multitude of problems and must embrace a range of interconnected, overlapping, and occasionally competing responses. We will not progress steadily toward a single solution to the problem of climate change; we must instead sustain multiple responses, some of which may seem hypocritical or contradictory, to the complexities of climate change over many generations for the foreseeable future.

Novelist Amitav Ghosh has proposed that the contemporary era might come to be known as the "Great Derangement," because most people are so unable to see the ways that climate change and global inequality prove fundamental claims of Enlightenment thinking false. Thus, in contrast to thinkers like Lomborg, he argues that the ideology of freedom and rationality has led to a world that constrains people to a less hospitable climate and irrationally unchecked degradation. He further argues with those who identify a singular cause for such derangement, particularly focusing on the ways that capitalism and empire intersect in complicated ways to create an unequal world of climate change.[24]

We extend Ghosh's argument even more broadly, insisting that derangement is inevitable whenever we seek to tell a single story about the complexities of the world. One of many lessons to be drawn from climate change is the danger of believing that the world responds predictably to our actions. The climate has changed because people acted with insufficient knowledge, altering their environments without adequate understanding of their workings, limits, and patterns. One of many causes of climate change is the frenetic activity of powerful people in industrialized societies who were certain that they were making progress. Thus, we argue, moral responses to climate change should avoid action without reflection and should be suspicious of urgent action with a singular goal. Responding to complexity takes time, and we must learn to face problems without pointing to a singular sociocultural cause or a clear solution. We must respond to climate change and the variety of other problems we face at the pace of ambiguity.

Toward a participatory environmental ethics

Climate change is a problem, and it is caused by—among other factors—consumption in the industrialized world, technological limitations, failures of global governance, and a lack of moral attention to the global atmosphere and the multitudinous creatures dependent upon it. And, of course, climate change is but one example of environmental degradation. Biodiversity in tropical rainforests is lost because of economic development, ineffective political and ecological management, the individual choices of many landowners, and anthropocentric assumptions about the relative importance of nonhuman species. The disproportionate burden of pollution placed on poor and marginalized peoples is a problem with roots in racism, colonialism, corporatization, and disenfranchisement. The instability of global and local food production and distribution is a problem caused in part by carelessness, industrialization, urbanization, and population growth. Of course, these are interconnected problems; but it is too simplistic to lump them all together. Indeed, it would be better to say that climate change, extinction, environmental injustice, and food insecurity are each, themselves, networks of interconnected, wicked environmental problems.

To phrase any or all of these challenges as a single problem is to elide the diversity of cultures and practices and individuals within humanity and the variety of scales and kinds of problems in human relationships to the nonhuman world. The idea of an "environmental crisis," like "environment," must be unpacked and complexified whenever it is used. This is the only way to honestly face what is really happening and carefully consider how we might respond.

As Jeffrey Ellis notes, essentialized approaches to environmental problems—taking the "silver bullet approach to understanding the global environmental crisis"—simply do not reflect reality. "The idea that there is a single root cause to any one of these problems, let alone to all of them taken together, is, to put it mildly, absurd. Because environmental problems are each the result of a multiplicity of causal factors, there can be no one comprehensive solution to all of them."[25] There is no silver bullet, nor a discrete monster at which to shoot it. Histories, biologies, religions, and sciences are multiperspectival, polydox, and hybrid in such a way that identifying a problem within one realm or discipline means ignoring the very real problems in other realms, with other names, from other directions. Multiple problems unfold across many boundaries in such a way that if we begin to tussle with one, the fabric of others will inevitably become unraveled. This is the "wickedness" of the wicked problems: In the process of

56

"solving" anything in this category, a whole new set of problems will always emerge.

Because we do not face a single problem, there is no straight line of progress toward a solution. The task of environmentalists is not to get to *the* answer to the environmental crisis, nor to urgently act in a single direction. Our task, instead, is to fully participate in the complexity of dialogue about what to do, taking cautious actions and adapting as the results of our actions and our dialogues continue unfolding. In this way, ethics becomes more ecological, more of a contextual interaction of multiple organisms and perspectives that flow in and out of one another toward an open, evolving future.

Ethicist James Gustafson offers a model for this approach. He begins with an idea familiar to most environmentalists—everything that exists is interconnected with everything else. However, the primary lesson of such interconnectedness for Gustafson is not the unity of all creation, nor a common narrative to be embraced by all cultures and all peoples. To the contrary, he argues, "Interdependence does not automatically issue in harmony of desired and desirable ends." Instead, "the multidimensionality of values, human and others, is the basis for relational values and for tensions between them." The interconnectedness of ecosystems, the planet, and the cosmos results in a reality that is too complicated for human beings to fully understand. This has moral implications, drawing "us into ambiguities of choices that are unavoidable."[26] So, environmentalists face a range of compelling goals—to mitigate climate change, to adapt to its effects, to defend marginalized peoples, to protect other species, to advance human health, and many more. The fact that these goals are interconnected does not necessarily mean that they are harmonious.

Indeed, sometimes the connections will be competitive, and difficult choices will be required. The work of convincing people that capitalism is a faulty global religion of overconsumptive destruction is valuable, but so is the work of convincing corporations and mainstream politicians to take small steps to regulate or tax carbon emissions within a capitalist economy. These two important projects may well be incompatible, and a choice may need to be made between them. Along similar lines, the work of developing new technologies to reduce carbon emissions and harvest energy in cleaner ways is important, but so is the work of convincing people that technological innovation is no panacea, and that increases in efficiency often lead to increases in consumption. Environmental ethics and environmental activism must be conducted amidst ambiguity, without a clear and simple direction. They must be conducted from within the cloud of unknowing which hangs over any place and time, a cloud that can also be pregnant with possibilities.[27]

These challenges call not for strident clarity but humble dialogue. Gustafson distinguishes between such stances as "prophetic" and "participatory," respectively. The prophet "stands with and for God over against the existing society and culture, over against the spiritual and moral ethos of his time and place.... He sees himself as God's appointed man in a society and culture estranged from

God and corrupted by its failure to obey God's commands."[28] The participant, by contrast, does not assume that she knows what the future should look like. The participant makes judgments as "one partner among many in the human conversation," prizing "the capacity to listen to and understand other points of view, to comprehend basic options thrust up by political, technological, and scientific developments, and to speak meaningfully and clearly."[29] The participant, in other words, does not claim to be exceptional or to hold any sort of moral high ground. Perhaps we need fewer heroes and prophets and more participants in the planetary community.

Most environmentalists tend toward prophetic discourse—decrying the unsustainability, cruelty, or carelessness of contemporary structures and declaring clear solutions. We advocate a more participatory stance, engaging in dialogue between diverse groups with competing goals. Effective dialogue requires the acknowledgment of multiple goals and agendas; it is stifled by any claim that there is a single right answer, a single correct direction. Sociologist Alexis Shotwell powerfully critiques what Gustafson calls prophetic discourse, noting that it leads to a focus on "purity," an attempt to cleanse ourselves of the bad things in the world rather than to try to make them better, to fool ourselves into believing that we can "meet and control a complex situation that is fundamentally outside our control." Shotwell calls, instead, for ethics that sounds more like participation, starting "from an understanding of our implication in this compromised world" as part of our desire "to act on our *wish that it were not so*."[30]

This participatory approach is compatible with historian Carolyn Merchant's partnership ethics, an approach she developed in opposition to what she calls stewardship or managerial ethics.[31] A steward or manager, like a prophet, assumes that some leader has the answers, knows what to do, and that everyone else should listen to this leader. By contrast, a partnership model, like a participatory ethic, emphasizes that the best possible responses to the challenges we face do not exist until diverse groups come together to consider them. Merchant's *Reinventing Eden* is a critique of narratives about progress and decline, arguing that these inherently lock us in to linear paths and simplistically rank any action as "good," or "bad." Such linear thinking does not map onto a chaotic world.[32]

Still another guide to participatory environmentalism is the philosopher Val Plumwood, who emphasizes the importance of interacting with multiple earth others. Rather than forcing a monological position onto other people and other species, Plumwood calls for a dialogical approach recognizing that the possibility of con/versation already implies an openness to learn from and be changed by the other's point of view or way of thinking.[33] Such interactions are messy and take time, but are essential tools to overcome what she calls "ecological irrationality," an attitude rooted in unquestioning assumptions that anthropocentrism, androcentrism, or any other singular way of thinking is adequate.

An ethics of ambiguity: process over progress

This book calls for an ethics of ambiguity, which can now be more clearly defined as participatory rather than prophetic, partnering rather than managerial, dialogical rather than monological. This is the ethics of "the idiot" advocated by Isabel Stengers and discussed in Chapter 1. In a world dominated by bold confidence, bigger-is-better, and snap judgments, it seems like idiocy to accept limits to our knowledge, conducting slow conversations across difference rather than acting monolithically. This is ethics at the pace of ambiguity: "the idiot demands that we slow down, that we don't consider ourselves authorized to believe we possess the meaning of what we know."[34]

For Stengers, the primary metaphor of moral deliberation is not a debate in which representatives struggle to articulate the desires of constituencies and hope to win over the opposition, but rather the palaver, a meandering and pointless conversation. The role of discussant is, "above all to remove the anesthesia produced by the reference to progress or the general interest."[35] A genuine dialogue creates room for agreement to emerge precisely because agreement is not assumed: "The common world must be free to emerge from the multiplicity of their disparate links."[36] The common world is not fully formed, it is emergent, and it must take into account the undercommons as discussed in Chapter 1, those voices that have been left out and damaged by past and current constructions of "commonality."[37] Unless and until it does, we must accept the ambiguity of knowing that we face serious problems but have no immediate solutions. In response to ambiguous problems, our progress will be, at best, ambiguous.

In a world of certainty, where problems have one clear answer, there are easily identified and defended rights and goods. In a world of simplistic progress, there is a clear direction in which to move, and every action either contributes to or detracts from such progress. If Leopoldian expansion is what environmental ethics requires, then it is right to extend our moral concern and it is progress when we convince others to do so as well. But the world of climate change is ambiguous: expansion of concern to include polar bears and Bangladeshis may well lead some to take action to mitigate climate change, but it also leads them to fly to the arctic to study bears or to Bangladesh to assist their neighbors. Such travel expands attention and awareness, but it also increases fossil fuel consumption and managerial attempts to "solve" climate change. It is as reasonable to argue that extending our attention outward is a problem as it is to call it a solution.

In a monological world of prophetic morality, one is either with or against the forces of progress. A prophetic approach to climate change identifies a villain—fossil fuel corporations or climate change deniers are popular targets—and rallies the faithful against them. They are destroying the world, and we must stop them. But "we" who care deeply about climate change sometimes fly in planes, drive in cars, and eat factory-farmed meat or commodity crops such as soy, corn, and palm oil. We may not deny the reality of climate change, but we likely neglect to insist upon it in every occasion. We may tweet out our support of climate activists, but we do so on phones and through an internet powered by a fossil fuel economy. In a world of clarity, these lapses could be called hypocritical. But that is not our world, and so such tension must be accepted as an inevitable reality: one can only participate in public discourse about climate change if one participates in the system that is changing the climate.

The common philosophical critique of moral ambiguity is that it becomes relativistic—once morality can be compromised, once right and wrong are muddied, there is no standard by which to judge good and evil. Everything is allowed and nothing is forbidden. If we are all complicit in the complex problem of climate change, then what incentive is there to change our behavior?

Our ethics of ambiguity indeed steers away from absolutes like "right" and "wrong" and "good" and "evil." These terms lend themselves to absolutism, to progressive thinking, to simplicity. But space remains for "better" and "worse," for analysis of whether ideas and actions are "constructive" or "destructive." For example, while we offer a friendly critique above, we find the analyses of Michael Northcott and Sallie McFague to be constructive in that they point to deep economic and political factors contributing to environmental degradation. While capitalism is not the singular cause of our problems and an alternative would not be a singular answer, it is important to analyze and explore the ways dominant institutions make continued climatic shifts possible. Such analysis is, in fact, essential to oppose the simplistic narrative of progress frequently propagated in mainstream culture. Thus, we believe Northcott and McFague's analyses, while imperfect, are better than Bjørn Lomborg and Ruth DeFries's, which more simplistically dismiss the complexity of climate change. The critique of capitalism and technology is more constructive than the defense. Neither has the whole truth—no one ever will—but the former reflects better and fuller participation.

Ambiguity is not an impediment to moral discernment; it is, instead, the impetus for moral engagement. In a world of right and wrong, one picks a side and then steps into line. In a world of better and worse, one must continually struggle to learn more, to develop nuanced awareness, and to act as well as possible. One never arrives at the correct, safe resting space, but continues to take account of the effects of thinking and acting, learn from others, and shift toward better and away from worse perceived possibilities in the world. An ethics of uncertainty admits that every action has inconceivable and unknown consequences because we are and always will be entangled, planetary creatures.[38]

Morality that leaves room for complexity is better than morality that assumes simplicity. But, of course, ambiguity itself is no ethical silver bullet. Other ethical standards like justice, responsibility, and care are still deeply important, and all are relevant to the problem of climate change. Our point is that none is sufficient by itself. An ethics that examines the complicated interplay between different ideals is more constructive than an ethics that focuses on only one.

Conclusion: ethics at the end of the world

Aldo Leopold introduced the idea of moral progress with a story from the heroic tale of Odysseus, a classic of Western literature about an iconic man's journey home. We suspect that the early 21st century calls for a different kind of narrative, less about a single hero's progress and more about a diverse community's questions. We suspect that we will find this not in a broad story about history, but from the speculative worlds of fiction.[39] Perhaps the next great insight into environmental ethics will be kicked off by an image from Cormac McCarthy's *The Road*, in which the company one keeps along the journey through a difficult world is more important than the direction in which one heads. Or perhaps a foundational insight can be found in Lois Lowry's *The Giver*, in which uniformity is a sign not of utopia but of dictatorial control, of people who have given up on the freedom of complexity and lost because of it. These two dystopian novels suggest the limits of progress, of quick solutions. Taking this perspective seriously means recognizing that the world some of us have hoped for is gone. If there was ever a world of simple progress, of straightforward moral expansion, of clarity, that world has ended. To accept that we do not live in that world is the vital first step for living morally in this one.

Along these lines, philosopher Timothy Morton argues that we are in fact living after the end of the world: the modern world of subjects as isolated agents and single grand narratives is past. We are now all part of much larger objects/subjects, and we cannot break away from these objects to see from above the fray. In other words, the world as we have been taught to know it is over. Perhaps it never existed.[40] We are not heading towards a utopia, nor are we apocalyptically leaving one.[41] Indeed, we may learn something from Indigenous Peoples and former slaves about life after the end of the world, as these peoples have lived in resilience and resistance despite the ends of their own worlds.[42]

There are, of course, reasons that environmentalists have tended toward apocalyptic, prophetic, managerial, and monological stances, insisting on immediate action and clear answers. Environmental problems are serious, deadly, and worsening. It only makes sense that most activists emphasize the necessity of clear problems and immediate action. A single problem for which a single answer can be developed is efficient, and it is faithful to the modern project of progress. But this is not a time for progress, it is a time for complexity. A complex world facing wicked problems does not afford the luxury of efficiency. We humans, in order to survive the changing climate, will have to stay with the troubled planet and its other inhabitants for a long time to come. We must learn to live in a world less perfect than that falsely painted by the myth of progress. The pace of solutions to our challenges—environmental and otherwise—simply will not be as straightforwardly progressive as we might like.

Ethics for the world after modernity should be participatory, it must emphasize partnership, and it must engage in genuine dialogue. Ethics for the world of climate change should counter the fast-paced technology- and market-driven world that helped to create the problem with a meandering, ambiguous pace of consideration. The problems are simply too big to be solved with the urgency of immediate, expansive action.

Such an ambiguous ethics is not brand new, and it becomes far easier to grasp its implications when it is brought into conversation with other activists. Thus, the next chapter turns to find constructive ambiguities in the writings and lives of Martin Luther King, Jr. and Malcolm X, whose social activism offer precedent and challenge for the ethics of ambiguity outlined here.

Notes

1 Leopold, *Sand County Almanac*, 237.
2 Ibid., 239.
3 Berry, *The Great Work*, 106. Berry's idea emerges from Teilhard de Chardin's belief that evolution is compelling humanity and all of the universe toward an "omega point".
4 Tal, *Speaking of Earth*, 258. The title of Maathai's speech is "The Challenge is to Restore the Home of the Tadpoles and Give Back to Our Children a World of Beauty and Wonder."
5 Savoy, *Trace*, Ch 3.
6 Yusoff, *A Billion Black Anthropocenes or None*, 24.
7 White, "Historical Roots of Our Ecologic Crisis."
8 For critiques of this misuse of White, see Bauman, "What's Left Out of the Lynn White Narrative;" Riley, "The Democratic Roots of our Ecologic Crisis;" and Jenkins, "After Lynn White."
9 Northcott, *The Environment and Christian Ethics*, 83.
10 Northcott, *A Moral Climate*, 165; Northcott, "The Concealment of Carbon Markets and the Publicity of Love in a Time of Climate Change," 294.
11 Northcott, *Environment and Christian Ethics*, 67–70.
12 McFague, *A New Climate for Theology*, 84.
13 McFague, *Life Abundant*, 81–85, 117.
14 Lomborg, *Skeptical Environmentalist*, 7, 351.
15 Lomborg, *Cool It*.
16 DeFries, *The Big Ratchet*.
17 Gore, *An Inconvenient Truth*, 100–101.
18 Quoted in Charles Clover, "Climate Change is Like 'World War Three'." *The Telegraph*, 2007.
19 Latour, *Down to Earth*, 90.
20 Bill McKibben has variously proposed the oil industry and carbon itself as the enemy in the "war" of climate change. (See "Global Warming's Terrifying New Math," *Rolling Stone*, August 2, 2012; and "A World at War," *The New Republic*, August 15, 2016.) For reflections on the dangers of such rhetoric, see O'Brien, "The 'War' Against Climate Change and Christian Eco-Justice."
21 Berry, *A Continuous Harmony*, 77.
22 Berry, *Citizenship Papers*, 17.
23 Beavan, *No Impact Man*, 6, 13.
24 Ghosh, *Great Derangement*.
25 Jeffrey C. Ellis, "On the Search for Root Cause: Essentialist Tendencies in Environmentalist Discourse," in Cronon, *Uncommon Ground*, 267.
26 Gustafson, *A Sense of the Divine*, 135, 68.

27 Keller, *Cloud of the Impossible*.
28 "The Theologian as Prophet, Preserver, or Participant," in Gustafson, *Theology and Christian Ethics*, 75. Gustafson's third type, the "preserver" who defends existing structures without critique, is not particularly relevant to our discussion since the environmentalist community is defined by a desire to change existing systems.
29 Ibid., 84–85.
30 Shotwell, *Against Purity*, 8, 204.
31 Merchant, *Reinventing Eden*.
32 Ibid.
33 Plumwood, *Environmental Culture*.
34 Stengers, "The Cosmopolitical Proposal," 995.
35 Ibid., 1003.
36 Ibid., 999.
37 Keller, *Political Theology of the Earth*.
38 See Keller, *Cloud of the Impossible*.
39 Two wise fiction writers have argued well that fiction has a pivotal role to play in encouraging people to participate in building a better world. See Ghosh, *The Great Derangement*, and Ursula Leguin, "Acceptance Speech," at the National Book Foundation Medal for Distinguished Contribution to American Letters, (November 20, 2014): http://www.ursulakleguin.com/Index-NBFMedal.html.
40 Morton, *Hyperobjects*.
41 Stenmark, "Developing an Apocalyptic Vision."
42 Bray, *Grave Attending*.

4

COMPLEXITY IN ACTION

The challenging uncertainties of Martin Luther King, Jr., and Malcolm X

The preceding chapter argued that complexity is more important than progress in contemporary moral arguments, and that environmentalism should prioritize participatory engagement over prophetic decrees, collaborative partnership over hierarchical stewardship, dialogue over monologue. A participatory ethics works at the pace of ambiguity rather than progress. These are not merely arguments about academic ethics, but also about environmental activism: urgently pushing toward progress in a singular direction does not address the complexities of the varied problems facing the environment and the globe. It is time for a more nuanced and honest struggle with the ambiguities of environmental degradation in the 21st century.

To develop and challenge this position, this chapter brings it into conversation with two of the most prominent and rhetorically powerful social activists of the 20th century: Malcolm X and Martin Luther King, Jr. Unlike the other conversation partners in this book, it is inappropriate to understand either King or X as an environmentalist. While both paid broad attention to global issues, they focused primarily on the violence of racial injustice and the moral goal of human rights; neither aligned himself in any way with the environmental movement. As such, they serve not as exemplars of environmental action, but rather of social activism more broadly. But their roles in the movements of the 1960s makes them uniquely influential in the history of social change in the United States. While neither achieved all the goals he set during his lifetime, both helped to drive significant cultural and legal transitions that deserve appreciation and can inspire anyone hoping to change the world. In short, King and X matter to environmentalism because they represent social movements from which we should learn.

Numerous environmentalists have already drawn connections between their cause and King's work. This is most explicit in the environmental justice movement, which frequently presents itself as the logical outgrowth and continuation of civil rights struggles. For example, ecowomanist ethicist Melanie Harris notes that King's final work was in support of a sanitation workers strike in Memphis, Tennessee, which was in part about standing up against the environmental and health hazards those workers were facing: "King grasped the connections between poverty, individual and institutional racism, and environmental health hazards, and he interpreted these as threats to justice."[1] Ethicist Hak Joon Lee makes a broader argument that King's moral vision is "capacious enough to address the problem of ecological injustice," and that his central ideas—"community, interdependence, respect for all life, and non-violence"—all "happen to be the core values of ecological ethics."[2]

The environmental potential of Malcolm X's thought is less explored, partly because he is less celebrated in popular culture and so the genius of his moral vision is less appreciated. But there is much to learn here, as is suggested when Hope Lewis begins her argument about human rights abuses against people of color in New Orleans after Hurricane Katrina by quoting Malcolm X's call for African Americans to "internationalize our problem."[3] X repeatedly linked domestic civil rights struggles to questions of human rights, international economics, and global citizenship. Furthermore, because he spent most of his public career as a black nationalist advocating independence and separation from dominant white society, he paid extensive attention to issues of physical geography, repeatedly emphasizing that racial minorities could only be free if they controlled their own land.[4] X not only modeled a captivating and powerfully influential approach to social activism, he also outlined an ethics that is useful and challenging for contemporary environmentalists, an ethics based on the belief that people who have suffered racism and oppression should "be given the rights of a human being in this society, on this earth, in this day, which we intend to bring into existence by any means necessary."[5]

When engaging the thinking of X and King, it is important to explicitly acknowledge one's own background and the goals one brings to reading them. The authors of this book come to the writings of these two activists as outsiders, distant not only in time but also in social location from X's and King's communities. We are ethnically white, born into and living in economic privilege and security. This informs and limits what we claim to understand from these men. We seek to learn from both, but we acknowledge that we have much more to learn and can only begin a conversation about how they might inform contemporary environmentalism, a conversation into which we invite all who read these words and a conversation that we fully expect will continue changing our minds and deepening our understanding. We certainly do not claim to be writing about what either King or X would say about contemporary ethics or environmental challenges—such claims, if ever appropriate, should not come from two white middle-class men. Rather, we are developing our own arguments after having worked to take seriously what Malcolm X and Martin Luther King, Jr., said about the challenges faced by their communities, in their times.

This chapter will engage the writings of King and X to identify and explore three lessons about contemporary environmental activism: 1) Ambiguity is inevitable, but it is not an excuse for inaction; 2) Hope is most possible when it is distinguished from a simplistic belief in progress, and 3) Meaningful action responding to complex social problems requires critical, pragmatic reflection.

Called to action: responding to real injustices

While much is made of the disagreements between Martin Luther King, Jr., and Malcolm X, it is worth beginning with a claim they shared in common: people of conscience are called to radical and immediate action in response to the world's injustice and violence. At the founding rally of the Organization of Afro-American Unity, which Malcolm X created in the last year of his life, he articulated this well: "We can never have peace and security as long as one black man in this country is being bitten by a police dog. No one in the country has peace and security."[6] King made a strikingly similar argument a year before with these words: "Injustice anywhere is a threat to justice everywhere. We are caught in an inescapable network of mutuality, tied in a single garment of destiny. Whatever affects one directly affects all indirectly."[7] Both men taught insistently and consistently that no one can separate herself from oppression: as long as anyone suffers, everyone is called to act.

This is as important today as it was in their time, as emphasized by the movement and persecution of black bodies by the justice system highlighted by the phrase Black Lives Matter. The refugee crises across the Western world, the persecution of refugees along the southern borders of the United States, and the continued denial of basic rights to Native American communities also suggest that injustice is not confined to any single race. This is part of the problem with narratives of progress: progress for whom? X's and King's rhetoric is indubitably, disturbingly applicable to our contexts today.

King and X's emphasis on action is also supremely relevant to the 21st century trends of climate change and globalized consumption. While the world is changing everywhere, the harm for such changes disproportionately harms the poor and people of color. Increasingly destructive weather patterns and shifting temperatures are most disruptive for those who have the fewest resources and benefit the least from industrial technologies causing the problems in the first place. Toxic wastes are disproportionately dumped into the neighborhoods and nations of marginalized groups. Environmental protections and social safety nets are disproportionately extended to wealthy peoples of European origin.[8] In short, the moral challenges of our century are shaped by white privilege, and anyone who takes the moral teachings of King and X seriously must respond with urgency to the violence and injustice of contemporary environmental and economic degradation.

This is a helpful test and corrective to the ethics of unknowing outlined in this book. Our call for a participatory morality at the pace of ambiguity is only justifiable if it can be consistent with calls to action from leaders like X and King. Both men directed harsh criticisms at "liberals" who claimed to support the cause of racial justice but dragged their feet and ultimately stood in the way. King's most famous encounter with such liberals occurred in Birmingham, Alabama, where he received a letter from eight Alabama clergymen after he had been jailed for civil disobedience. They asked him to end his protests in the city. This request began by agreeing with King's goals in broad strokes, acknowledging "racial friction and unrest," and applauding the desire to work "peacefully for a better Birmingham." But they also asked King to leave the city and end his "unwise and untimely" action, favoring the more gradual and less disruptive process of legislative and judicial change.[9] King responded with one of his most powerful pieces of writing, the "Letter from Birmingham Jail." Citing his and other African Americans' experiences of racism and oppression, he develops a withering argument against his critics:

> Perhaps it is easy for those who have never felt the stinging darts of segregation to say, 'Wait.' But when you have seen vicious mobs lynch your mothers and fathers at will and drown your sisters and brothers at whim; when you have seen hate-filled policemen curse, kick, and even kill your black brothers and sisters; when you see the vast majority of your twenty million Negro brothers smothering in an airtight cage of poverty in the midst of an affluent society; when you suddenly find your tongue twisted and your speech stammering as you seek to explain to your six-year-old daughter why she can't go to the public amusement park that has just been advertised on television, and see tears welling up in her eyes when she is told that Funtown is closed to colored children, and see ominous clouds of inferiority beginning to form in her little mental sky, and see her beginning to distort her personality by developing an unconscious bitterness toward white people. ... Then you will understand why we find it difficult to wait.[10]

King went on to express his disappointment in moderates who agreed with his cause but encouraged him to be more patient about achieving his goals, arguing that this reveals "a tragic misconception of time, from the strangely rational notion that there is something in the very flow of time that will inevitably cure all ills." Dismissing any sense of inevitability, King countered: "We must use time creatively, in the knowledge that the time is always ripe to do right."[11] He titled the book in which this letter was published *Why We Can't Wait*, and his perspective serves as a powerful argument that those who care about justice must always stand up and take action.[12]

Malcolm X offers a similarly withering critique of those who claimed to support his goals but asked him to slow the process of reaching them. In his autobiography, X recounts the story of a teacher who discouraged him from pursuing a career as a lawyer, cautioning him, "Malcolm, one of life's first needs is for us to be realistic... . A lawyer, that's no realistic goal for a [racial slur]. You need to think about something you *can* be. You're good with your hands—make things." X notes that he believes this teacher meant well, but goes on to say "the more I thought afterwards about what he said, the more uneasy it made me. It just kept treading around in my mind." This incident led to his disengagement from school and from white culture more broadly, and fed the separatist black nationalism that characterized most of his public career. Throughout his life, X continued to offer harsh criticisms of well-meaning and "realistic" white liberals. He later called white liberals "the world's worst hypocrites," who tended to be more interested in telling African Americans how to conduct their protests than in truly listening to and learning from the experience of racism's victims and survivors.[13]

The pace of ambiguity discussed in this book is only valid if it can be distinguished from the waiting that King criticized in the well-meaning clergy of Birmingham. The complexity advocated here should only be compelling if it is something diametrically opposed to the "realism" that led X's teacher to discourage a brilliant student's intellect and ambition. The sections below attempt to make this case, and then to use the complex relationship between King and X to further support the importance of unknowing in environmental activism.

Dreams and nightmares: Martin Luther King, Jr., and the precariousness of progress

King is rightly remembered and celebrated for his profound hope that human beings, the United States of America, and the world could be better. Raised in a violently divided and oppressive society, he nevertheless imagined a future of peaceful community and justice. These ideas are best known from the keynote address he gave at the 1963 March on Washington, in which he shared his dream that "my four little children will one day live in a nation where they will not be judged by the color of their skin but by the content of their character," and that "one day every valley shall be exalted, every hill and mountain shall be made low, the rough places shall be made plain, and the crooked places shall be made straight and the glory of the Lord will be revealed and all flesh shall see it together."[14] Most who cite King in the 21st century reference this optimistic King of dreams.

Such dreaming is a vital resource for contemporary environmentalism, which can too easily become grimly resigned to the worst possible futures. With waters rising and extreme weather events increasing, it is easy to wallow in the troubling realities of the status quo. With political leaders far behind their people when it comes to the realities and urgency of this problem, it is easy to despair. As ethicist Anna Peterson argues, contemporary activists need utopian thinking that imagines a better future, "believing that there are always alternatives, that better worlds are always possible."[15] King's dream offers a hopeful counter to gloom and doom.[16]

However, as anyone who takes King's entire legacy seriously knows, his dream for the future did not always make him optimistic, and the five years he survived after the famous 1963 speech provided many frustrations and perils that challenged his utopian hope.[17] Consider his words from a Christmas sermon in 1967:

> not long after talking about that dream I started seeing it turn into a nightmare… as I moved through the ghettos of the nation and saw my black brothers and sisters perishing on a lonely island of poverty in the midst of a vast ocean of material prosperity, and saw the nation doing nothing to grapple with the Negroes' problem of poverty.[18]

The dream was real, but so was the nightmare; the latter revealed how difficult and painful it would be to reach the former. King saw his dream as increasingly distant as he became more acquainted with economic injustices, with the sin of militarism that his nation was perpetrating in Vietnam, and with racism as a global phenomenon. This is a vital lesson for any activist: even if the ideal may be clear, the path toward it is fraught and complicated; obstacles and diversions are inevitable, success never is.

Indeed, King's framing of his hope as a "dream" itself suggests this caution. Standing in front of the Lincoln Memorial, King did not claim to have a plan or a promise, but a dream of what could be, "one day." Dreams are inherently ambiguous and require interpretation; dreams are intimations rather than certainties. King's hope was framed to avoid certainty—a dream rather than a concrete prediction—and to inspire action—a project to work on rather than a promise to wait on. He offered no guarantee of success, but rather a hope against the stiflingly oppressive realities faced by his community. While it is tempting to reduce King's dream to a simplistic hope for a less segregated society, he looked instead for a world that was truly fair, free from prejudice, from violence, and from poverty. The world King dreamed of has not arrived; he was articulating a vision of the future that is simultaneously more revolutionary and less clear than most interpreters assume.

Kingian dreaming, inherently ambiguous, is a powerful resource for 21st century environmentalism. We know that climate change and globalization will alter our world in ways that we cannot even imagine, and so we must find ways to hope, working toward the best future we can imagine. All bets are off, certainty gives way to ambiguity and multiple possibilities, and this is fertile ground for the kind of hope King modeled, sprouting outrage and action in the face of uncertainty.

Throughout his public career, King was aware that dreams require interpretation and development, that good news is never unambiguous. In his book *Strength to Love*, he applied this lesson to the idea of progress with a theological slant, arguing that "All progress is precarious, and the solution of one problem brings us face to face with another problem. The Kingdom of God as a universal reality is *not yet*. Because sin exists on every level of man's existence, the death of one tyranny is followed by the emergence of another tyranny."[19] He observed many signs of hope in U.S. history: the creation of democracy, the Emancipation Proclamation, the end of colonialism, *Brown vs. Board of Education*. He celebrated each one. But, he noted, none of these was a complete victory. Emancipation may have ended legal slavery, but it led to new kinds of oppression in the era of Reconstruction.[20] All progress is precarious; success may come, but we can never expect it to be unambiguously good and we should never plan on an end to the struggle.

The same point is made powerfully in an account of the structural racism of 21st century mass incarceration, Michelle Alexander's *The New Jim Crow*. Alexander demonstrates that prisons in the United States are a tool of white supremacy, noting that "racism is highly adaptable." The defeat of slavery led to the new violence of segregationist laws, and that the collapse of explicit segregation has led to more subtle but still destructive systems like the disproportionate incarceration of African Americans.[21] Racism adapts, as does every other form of violence and injustice, and so no form of resistance and no victory is ever complete.

King explained this reality with theological anthropology: human beings are always capable of evil as well as good, of acting out nightmares as well as dreams. When asked in 1965 to reflect on his mistakes, he focused on the temptation to blind optimism: "The most pervasive mistake I have made was in believing that because our cause was just, we could be sure that the white ministers of the South, once their Christian consciences were challenged, would rise to our aid... . I ended up, of course, chastened and disillusioned."[22] Having hoped that the natural goodness of other people would bring them to his cause, King was reminded that human beings are more complicated. As he put it in an early essay, "there is a strange dichotomy of disturbing dualisms within human nature... . Man has the capacity to be good, man has the capacity to be evil."[23] Experiencing this strange dichotomy, he increasingly insisted that protesters must demonstrate their power, make their opponents uncomfortable, and demand rather than simply ask for justice and equality.

For King, the dichotomy in human nature taught an important lesson not only about segregationists, but also about civil rights protestors—he understood all people, himself included, as flawed and capable of evil. Indeed, he argued against other pacifists who claimed to have right unambiguously on their side, emphasizing that those who admit moral dilemmas are more trustworthy than those who claim to have achieved moral purity.[24] King's hope was not a naïve trust in people to do what is right, but rather a sophisticated belief that good is possible if activists remain cautiously aware of the tendency for evil in themselves as well as their opponents. He put it personally in a 1966 address to the staff of the Southern Christian Leadership Conference: "I wanted to assure you that I am still searching myself. I don't have all the answers ... if there is anything about nonviolence that I accept absolutely it is the fact that it is an experiment with truth."[25]

King came to this cautious uncertainty through a theology he learned in the black church that insists all people are both made in the image of God and marked by sin. However, this approach is by no means unique to the Christian tradition. King also learned it from the works of Mohandas Gandhi, who entitled his autobiography "The Story of my Experiments with Truth" and emphasized that he was always learning to wrestle with the multiple sides of his own self and others'.[26] A similar lesson could certainly be derived from the interconnected and impermanent nature of human beings in Buddhism, trickster figures in indigenous traditions, and the moral complexity of the Patriarchs in Hebrew Scriptures. Religious traditions have few unambiguous lessons about good and evil, and King is one example of a person of faith wrestling against naïve certainty in goodness and progress, refusing to ignore the complicity and complexity of reality.[27]

King's theological background prepared him for the hard truth that progress is always precarious. The black church that nurtured him has, over centuries, developed a particular kind of hope in the face of the undeniable pain and degradation of chattel slavery, segregation, and cultural colonialism: hope while living through multiple apocalypses. In the face of those horrors, many African American Christians established a basic belief that the universe is ruled by "a creator God whose nature is fundamentally love."[28] King's hope came from faith in this God, and his ethics was based on a belief that he should work to imitate God's love and an acceptance that human beings would always fall short of it.

It seems reasonable to suggest that King's activism reflected not the certainty of progress, but the cautious and constant self-assessment of what we have called the pace of ambiguity. Perhaps the best demonstration of this approach comes from a quote King frequently repeated: "the arc of the moral universe is long but it bends toward justice."[29] King used this cosmological assertion to demand action, calling all who heard him to bend ourselves to the shape of the universe and help move it in the direction of justice for which it was created. But his emphasis that this arc is "long" makes it clear that the destination is not immediately before us. Perhaps the place we hope to go is centuries or millennia ahead of us, or perhaps it will look drastically different when we have moved further along the curve of the cosmos. Such an epic understanding of change reflects the pace of ambiguity rather than progress.

Learning from King: contemporary environmentalism at the pace of ambiguity

Many contemporary environmentalists frame their goal in clear and simplistic terms: sustainability, harmony with nature, or an ecozoic era are goals that are sometimes articulated in ways that sound as if the destination is clear and near at hand. A common assumption holds that if the general public simply understood the reality of environmental degradation, all necessary action would neatly and straightforwardly follow. Consider the popular plans published by the Earth Policy Institute focused on "Rescuing a Planet Under Stress" and "Mobilizing to Save Civilization." In his preface to the 2008 edition of the Institute's *Plan B 3.0*, Lester Brown emphasizes that human beings know enough to diagnose and solve the problems we face: "We have the technologies to restructure the world energy economy and stabilize climate. The challenge now is to build the political will to do so. Saving civilization is not a spectator sport."[30] Brown's call to action is admirable, but it assumes a high degree of certainty. He articulates not a dream but a plan, confidently asserting a path to progress. Perhaps he could learn from Martin Luther King, Jr., the dreamer who faced the nightmarish complexity of reality and morality head-on.[31]

71

King was profoundly aware that all human knowledge is fragile and partial. This includes even—or perhaps especially—knowledge that comes from attitudes of certainty, power, and privilege. The ways African American communities endured and overcame tragedies for centuries taught King the importance of action in the face of uncertainty.[32] Despite the enormous indeterminacy and open-endedness of each life and each community, every human being acts in the world, every decision either perpetuates or changes the world around us. The courage to act toward a different possible future emerges out of King's dreaming, hope-filled, uncertain space. By contrast, the white liberals who told King how to run his movement projected a certainty, believing they could dictate the pace of progress. The pace of ambiguity is, instead, about acting while fully aware of uncertainty.

King was masterful at creating and marshalling political will, but constantly reminds any student of his legacy how difficult that project is and how many questions are left unanswered even when one can get people working together. Segregationists did not simply give up once the moral argument against their cause was lost; indeed, at the time of this writing King's nation is still struggling to understand the ways racism is expressed against black bodies in violent acts committed by agents of the state. Environmentalists must learn the same lesson about those who today make the world warmer, less sustainable, and more impoverished. Those who cause destruction will not easily give it up.

This last point is especially important given the fact that all privileged citizens of the industrialized world—including the authors of this book—are part of the environmental problem. The choices we make deplete resources, degrade ecosystems, and contribute to climate change. Environmental ethics in our context is inevitably the work of people who contribute to environmental degradation. Those of us in the industrialized world with some measure of control over our lives and resources are born into a set of systems and unearned privileges that unjustly distribute human flourishing and ignore costs to other persons and to nonhuman systems.[33] In our time, the lives of privileged peoples are predisposed toward the degradation of the planet. King is again useful here: just as he reminded nonviolent protestors that they, too, were caught in networks of sinful violence, he offers a precedent for environmentalists to admit and accept that we are complicit in the systems we protest.

It is always tempting to prophetically believe that degradation is caused by an easily delineated group and can be healed by another easily delineated group. For example, Naomi Klein argues that climate change is proof that the political left has been correct and the political right has been wrong about just about everything. Asserting that unfettered free markets have caused and exacerbated global warming, she writes: "Climate change detonates the ideological scaffolding on which contemporary conservatism rests." The issue "implies the biggest political 'I told you so' since Keynes predicted German backlash from the Treaty of Versailles" and so "a green-left worldview, which rejects mere reformism and challenges the centrality of profit in our economy, offers humanity's best hope of overcoming these overlapping crises."[34] There is much to learn from Klein's analysis and politics, but the argument of this book is strongly against her rhetorical approach. She establishes a clear "us" and a "them" and chooses a side; she marks out a goal and insists that progress can only occur through linear movement toward it. Klein knows what a proper response to climate change looks like—more national and international regulation of fossil fuels that vastly decreases their use—and she shows little doubt that those who work for this goal are doing good while those who stand in its way are doing evil.[35]

King models a humbler approach, not staking out a clear standard of progress and not assuming that all good ideas will come from one group nor that all the damage will come from the other. This is where King's dream remains important: he hoped not that his side would win, but that a community would come together, surmounting disagreement to achieve a higher synthesis and unity. This demonstrates the ideal of the participatory ethic discussed in the previous chapter.[36] King's dream was not that the world would move in a direct line towards progress as he understood it. His dream was far more radical and precarious, that a new world could emerge for all. Environmentalists who seek to learn from King should seek similar dreams.

The challenge of the truth: Malcolm X and the rhetoric of critical opposition

In the middle of the turbulent 1960s, Malcolm X told Alex Haley, the co-author of his autobiography: "Let's just face truth. Facts! Whether or not the white man of the world is able to face truth, and facts, about the true reasons for his troubles—that's what essentially will determine whether or not *he* will survive."[37] Such commitment to truth and faith in its power are fundamental to X's personality and his public career. He devoted his life to helping people understand truths that had been buried by destructive customs and institutions. He also began to boldly imagine how to resist such dishonest structures. Studying X reveals a clear distinction between his resolute commitment to truth and the unimaginative realism that led his teacher to discourage his aspirations. That distinction is vital for an ethics of unknowing, helping to define the parameters of a constructively complex approach to environmental ethics.

Malcolm X's life was lived in a commitment to truth and a fundamental distrust of dishonesty and hypocrisy. He left school because he detected a dishonest hypocrisy in racist structures that rewarded less intelligent white students. He left the Christian faith of his parents because he saw hypocrisy among Christians who would preach freedom while thoughtlessly throwing people into prison, preach peace while justifying lynching, preach justice while propping up racist structures.[38] X distanced himself from King's branch of the civil rights movement because he saw hypocrisy in committing to nonviolence while asking for constitutional recognition from a government "that will go to war at the drop of a hat to defend itself."[39] In a sense he learned the "art of failure," in the face of systems that inherently rewarded injustice.[40] In every case, he sought honesty and consistency. The faith at the heart of this commitment is signaled in the final two sentences of his autobiography: "If I can die having brought any light, having exposed any meaningful truth that will help to destroy the racist cancer that is malignant in the body of America—then, all of the credit is due to Allah. Only the mistakes have been mine."[41]

X's commitment to truth came in part from his Muslim faith. The core tenet of this religion—there is no God but God—taught him that people are ultimately united by one fact: all are created by and should obey the same God. He therefore believed all those who "bow down to the one God, Allah, automatically accept each other as brothers and sisters, regardless of differences in complexion."[42] X did not commonly use the Arabic word *tawhid*, which captures the fundamental unity and uniqueness of the God who created all else, but this was nevertheless a basic inspiration for his critical analysis and his commitment to truth. The God of Islam is free of and separate from human prejudices and divisions. Before the one God, all people are simply human beings. After his conversion to Islam, X tested everything he heard against this basic truth and critiqued every distraction from it. Egyptian literature scholar Abdel Wahab Elmessiri argues that Islam offered X the "visionary frame of reference that liberated him from the racist assumptions of his society," and thereby gave him a standard "free from human prejudices and false distinctions."[43]

Malcolm X learned this theology originally from the Nation of Islam, but his autobiography narrates the way a break from that group led to even deeper commitment to truth. After years as a follower of Elijah Muhammad, X learned that his mentor had committed multiple acts of adultery and came to believe that the same man was conspiring to have him killed. Malcolm X found a bedrock of his belief system shaken. He captures the experience powerfully: "I felt as though something in *nature* had failed, like the sun, or the stars. It was that incredible phenomenon to me—something too stupendous to conceive." However, this experience was ultimately liberating because, through it, "I became able finally to muster the nerve, and the strength, to start facing the facts, to think for myself."[44]

Malcolm X's public career was devoted to similarly helping his audiences to think for themselves, spreading truth and nurturing habits of critique against what he saw as a widespread cultural program of misinformation. In an interview, he explained that racial prejudice is caused by "ignorance and greed. And a skillful program of miseducation that goes right along with the American system of exploitation and oppression."[45] The dominant society taught a falsely Euro-centric version of world history and philosophy, training African Americans to believe in their own inferiority and encouraging whites to embrace an unearned feeling of superiority. X deconstructed this narrative and taught his audience to question the assumptions it nurtured.

One of the most powerful lessons in critical thinking that Malcolm X offers is his name. Upon conversion to the Nation of Islam, he ceased to be Malcolm Little and became Malcolm X, in part to clearly break away from the name "imposed upon my paternal forebears" by a slave owner. Replacing his last name with "X" symbolized the fact that no one would ever know the "true

African family name" that had been taken from him.[46] By making his surname an unidentifiable variable, X demanded that everyone who encountered him reckon with the racist structures that had removed his ancestor's and his people's heritage.[47] Late in his life, after a pilgrimage in the Middle East, he also adopted the name el-Hajj Malik el-Shabazz, but he continued to be primarily known as "Malcolm X." We refer to him this way, and cite him by the surname "X," to honor the message he sent with his public name, which was that white supremacy had sought to take his family's true heritage from them. This is an example of Malcolm X's commitment to the truth and of how deeply he challenged others to recognize and face it.

Throughout his public career, X gave powerful speeches that aimed to liberate his listeners by educating them, offering an empowering history and a set of tools for critical thinking that he believed could set people free. This was most explicit in the weekly meetings he ran for his Organization of Afro-American Unity throughout 1964. He told his audiences that their task was "to go into our problem, and just analyze and analyze and analyze; and question things that you don't understand." The goal was not to offer clear answers to injustice, but instead to encourage people to think for themselves: "I, for one, believe that if you give people a thorough understanding of what it is that confronts them, and the basic causes that produce it, they'll create their own program; and when people create their own program, you get action."[48]

Rhetorical scholar Robert Terrill notes that X's speeches—particularly those delivered after he left the Nation of Islam and so spoke for himself rather than Elijah Muhammad—demonstrated for his listeners "tactics of judgment and critique that do not *lead toward* liberation so much as they *are* a liberation from the constraints and norms of the dominant culture."[49] Terrill defines X's rhetorical style in contrast to the prophetic—which assumes a coherent community and a clear path forward. Instead, he characterizes X's speaking as "oppositional prudence," inviting diverse audiences to become "active critics of the dominant culture, able to make independent judgments on it" rather than simply accepting the judgments of a speaker.[50] This is a deconstructive method through and through, apophatic in its understanding of reality but acknowledging what reality cannot be. While Martin Luther King, Jr., dreamed that his nation could achieve its dream of true equality, X oppositionally and prudently questioned whether the United States was a coherent community at all and whether the goals set out in its constitution were worth aspiring to.[51]

X provides a powerful model of participatory ethics. His moral system depends not upon simple directions or distinctions, but rather hard questions, critiques, and explorations. He powerfully articulated this kind of ethic in an interview when he insisted: "I think all of us should be critics of each other. Whenever you can't stand criticism you can never grow…. I don't think that we should be above criticism. I don't think that anyone should be above criticism."[52]

These words affirm the ethical argument of the previous chapter, but they also challenge it. An ambiguous environmental ethic is only justifiable against the standard X sets if it genuinely makes room for broad, dialogical criticism, raising awareness of its own limits as well as the limits of mainstream environmentalism and previous environmental thought. The ethics of unknowing articulated here seeks to live up to that standard, calling for an environmentalism that stirs audiences to oppose degrading systems by thinking for themselves rather than following any simplistic program.

Learning from X: toward a critically oppositional environmentalism

Perhaps the most prominent citizen organization currently leading the global response to climate change is 350.org, originally founded by Bill McKibben and a group of students from Middlebury College, which has since grown substantially and had enormous success coordinating global consciousness-raising campaigns, advocating fossil fuel divestment, and helping to coordinate international climate protests. The organization's name comes from the parts-per-million of CO_2 that would be compatible with limiting the global temperature shift to 2°C, a standard that they trace to the work of climate scientist James Hansen.[53] These two numbers—350 parts per million of CO_2 to ensure no more than 2° of warming—were widely accepted and embraced in the environmental movement and in international climate negotiations when the organization was founded.

Malcolm X's call to critically analyze all received wisdom encourages us to question what is widely accepted and embraced. A 2014 article by James Hansen revises his view to say that 2° would be disastrous, and suggests that 1° of warming is the most that the global system can handle without serious consequences.[54] Even more importantly, the leaders of many economically poor nations along the equator—who already experience extensive disruption from climate change and would experience more changes as the world warmed 2°—have raised profound objections to this standard. At the 2009 global climate talks in Copenhagen, the Sudanese diplomat Lumumba Di-Aping spoke against the 2° standard on behalf of 77 so-called "developing" countries. He began his speech by telling the other delegates, "We have been asked to sign a suicide pact," and insisted, "I would rather die with my dignity than sign a deal that will channel my people into a furnace."[55] This demonstrates the truth-telling fundamental to any reasonable ethical response to climate change. And it had an impact: the global community set 1.5° as a goal at the Paris climate talks in 2016. Since then, the Intergovernmental Panel on Climate Change (IPCC) has produced a report on how such a goal might be possible, which makes it clear that major political, economic, and technological change would be required.[56]

Neither the Paris Accord nor the IPCC set a clear goal of how many parts per million of CO_2 would be required to reach this goal, and so it remains a murkier and less clear aspiration than the earlier, very clear goal of 350 ppm to stay below 2°. It is likely for this reason that, at the time of this writing, 350. org continues to espouse the goal of limiting warming to 2°.[57] This is a comprehensible, potentially attainable goal.

By contrast, people like Lumumba Di-Aping and James Hansen insist on fully facing the complexities of our planet's challenging situation. The goals of 1° or 1.5° are less clear and less attainable. In opposition to the reductionist realism of those who seek a manageable goal, an ethics of unknowing calls for truth-telling, recognizing how far we are from a clear goal and then carefully considering how to respond to that reality. This follows in the tradition of Malcolm X, telling the truth no matter what.

Malcolm X insisted on telling the story of white supremacy and the harm it has caused. Along similar lines, perhaps the primary responsibility for environmentalists is not to set a concrete target for the future but to honestly recount present realities and the history that created them. In his book, *Slow Violence and the Environmentalism of the Poor*, literary scholar Rob Nixon notes that climate change inflicts pain upon poor and marginalized people so slowly that the world has been able to ignore it. He particularly emphasizes the example of the Maldives, a low-lying archipelago in the Indian Ocean that is likely to be the first nation eradicated by rising seas as the climate changes: "The island of Atlantis, according to Plato, vanished into the ocean 'in a single day and night of misfortune.' The engulfment threatening the Maldive Islands is nothing as unambiguously instantaneous as that."[58] In the face of such slow violence, Nixon lifts up the work of "writer-activists," charged with "drawing to the surface—and infusing with emotional force—submerged stories of injustice and resource rebellions,"[59] submerged stories that make up the "undercommons." Those concerned about the Maldives have no power to save it with a simple choice—the world is too ambiguous for that. But concerned people have an urgent responsibility to seek the truth, to tell the story in such a way that the world will pay attention, acknowledging the violence and injustice of climate change.

We will never live in a world without climate change. As Clive Hamilton puts it, "we can no longer prevent global warming that will this century bring about a radically transformed world that is much more hostile to the survival and flourishing of life."[60] Hamilton argues, therefore, that environmentalists must honestly face the destruction of ecosystems and human habitats. Reasonable action will only be possible after people face the truth. Human beings cannot solve climate change, and only by admitting that can we begin to address it. Malcolm X offers profound resources for facing the depth of these truths. Far more than most, he faced the violence and the injustices of segregation and the legacy of slavery, and he insisted that every audience he spoke to should wrestle with the truths of these horrors.

For most of his public career, X was a black nationalist who sought to lead African Americans back to Africa, to undo the crime of slavery and to put an ocean between his people and their white oppressors. This was an enormous goal, and one he knew was not likely to be met in the near term, but he nevertheless insisted that his people should have the right and the resources to return to the continent from which their ancestors had been taken. In insisting upon this, he helped his audiences to reckon with the violence of slavery and segregation, to recognize the depth of the divide in U.S. society. He demonstrates an oppositional insistence on the truth.

X was also a deeply pragmatic thinker, and this meant that he thought strategically about the distance between his goal and reality. At a rally of the Organization of Afro-American Unity, he made this clear:

> I want to go back to Africa. But what can I do while I'm waiting to go? Go hungry? Live in a rat-infested slum? Send my children to a school where their brains are being crippled? No, if we are going to go but time is going to pass between now and our going, then we have to have a long-range program and a short-range program, one that is designed to turn us in that direction, but at the same time one that is designed to enable us to take maximum advantage of every opportunity under this roof where we are right now.[61]

He articulates an example of what living in the midst of and through the end of the world might mean. Environmentalists who learn from this example should acknowledge that, just as whites in the U.S. can never undo the horrible violence of slavery and segregation, wealthy people cannot undo the emissions and industrialization that have already changed the climate. But this truth should not stop anyone from stating bold aspirations. We should seek a world with all remaining fossil fuels left in the ground, an international system that genuinely restricts carbon emissions to limit climate change to 1°, and an accounting of climate debts in which the rich and privileged pay reparations to those who did not benefit from climate changing emissions but suffer the most for them now. Such clearly stated goals allow us to honestly see both what positive change would look like and how far we are from an ideal world. Honestly facing these truths is essential to a dialogical, partnership ethic. X's proposal for "a long-range program and a short-range program" calls for responding to the immediate needs of climate refugees and the world's poor while working toward the distant—perhaps impossible—dream of a world where anthropogenic climate change is completely repaired. Anyone who seeks to respect the rights of human beings "in this society, on this earth, in this day" must first face the truth.

Divergent paths and uncertain legacies

Our participatory ethic aspires to match the oppositional critique Malcolm X demonstrated in the face of racial prejudice. The pace of ambiguity we advocate attempts to reflect the cautious hope Martin Luther King, Jr., modeled with his belief that the universe bends toward justice beyond human understanding. Ultimately, we believe these moral guidelines are compatible with one another and that both push toward an urgent but ambiguous response to the travails of earth and its inhabitants.

However, the disagreements between X and King also helpfully demonstrate the inevitability of ambiguity. X often sought to empower his movement and challenge his oppressors by referring to white people as "devils" and insisting that African Americans could only be free when they governed themselves. King, by contrast, taught his people to love their enemies and sought to convince white U.S. citizens that they could live in community with African Americans. King taught that the beloved community could only be reached through nonviolent means, and so emphasized the power of Gandhian methods. X asserted that the end of justice should be sought "by any means necessary," and dismissed as ridiculous any claim that African Americans should not defend themselves against violent aggression. X spent the last year of his life appealing to the international community to force the United States to recognize its own citizen's human rights. King remained committed to the constitution of the United States and a hope that national politics could make positive change.

These differences remain real and relevant 50 years after X and King were assassinated, and they demonstrate the complexity of any moral program. While both men struggled valiantly against racial injustice, they had notably different strategies and tactics. This diversity was in many ways a strength— King's political work was more effective because Malcolm X was seen by many whites as a dangerous alternative, and X's rhetoric was strengthened by the contrast he could draw with what he saw as King's compromises. Furthermore, precisely because of their differences, they learned an enormous amount from each other and broadened national attention to racial injustice.[62]

Perhaps the most striking aspect of the disagreements between Martin Luther King, Jr., and Malcolm X is that each believed the other to be insufficiently radical. X frequently called King out by name, dismissing him as "the best weapon that the white man, who wants to brutalize Negroes, has ever gotten in this country … because King has put this foolish philosophy out—you're not supposed to fight or you're not supposed to defend yourself."[63] For X, King was an example of the fundamental mistake of the civil rights movement, which accepted that "the American stage is a white stage. So a black man standing on that stage in America automatically is in the minority. He is the underdog, and in his struggle he always uses an approach that is a begging, hat-in-hand, compromising approach."[64]

While he never publicly critiqued X, King frequently distinguished his approach from that of black nationalists more generally, critiquing those who tried to "go out and whip the world" as fundamentally ineffectual. Like the white moderates who called him to wait, black nationalists "accomplish nothing; for they do not reach the people who have a crying need to be free."[65] King emphasized political action as an alternative to the unending cycles of violence, and believed that activists like Malcolm X who refused to engage in politics and to decry violence were simply feeding the flames of injustices they claimed to be fighting.

Each man believed that the other was caught in the problem, complicit and therefore insufficiently radical. They were both right and both wrong. Similarly, environmentalists today spend time arguing about what approach will most effectively and radically respond to the degradation of the planet and human communities. Some hope for a revolution in values in which people turn away from destructive technologies and embrace more pastoral ways of life; others hope for revolutionary technologies that will make globalized life and cities sustainable. Some hope for a radical change in self-understanding by which human beings learn to recognize ourselves as fully communing with all other life-forms; others hope for a radical form of justice that will deepen commitments to human rights and human equality. Some believe that religious tradition is essential for moral transformation away from secular consumption, others believe that truly new and more scientifically informed moral thinking is required in response to the new challenges of our time. There is no singular vision of an environmental future. All these ideas are radical in their own way, and none is clearly correct. Just as we have much to learn from both Martin Luther King, Jr., and Malcolm X, environmentalists have much to learn from the diversity within our own ranks.

The environmental movement in the 21st century must embrace not only ideological diversity but also diversities of race, ethnicity, geography, gender, sexuality, and belief. This will not lead to simplistic harmony, but instead to overlapping, conflicting, and competing goals and methods. Such ambiguous complexity is the only reasonable and productive response to challenges as large and as wicked as those facing human communities and our planet in our time. There is no one standard by which to measure environmental success, there is no single goal toward which to progress, and there is no single answer to our challenges. This is ultimately freeing, because it makes room for a morality that accepts ambiguity and embraces diversity, it calls for an ethics of unknowing.

Notes

1 Harris, *Ecowomanism*, 25. See also Bullard, *Quest for Environmental Justice*, 19.
2 Lee, *The Great World House*, 62. For another account of how King's witness is useful for the climate movement, see O'Brien, *Violence of Climate Change*, Ch. 6.
3 Lewis, "Race, Class, and Katrina," 233.
4 See especially Tyner, *The Geography of Malcolm X*.
5 X & Breitman, *By Any Means Necessary*, 56.
6 Ibid., 39.
7 King, *Why We Can't Wait*, 77.
8 See especially Bullard, et al., "Toxic Wastes and Race at Twenty;" Bullard, *Quest for Environmental Justice*; Moe-Lobeda, *Resisting Structural Evil*; Bauman, Bohannon, & O'Brien, *Inherited Land*, Ch. 9; and Cone, "Whose Earth is it, Anyway?"
9 C. C. J. Carpenter, et al., "Public Statement by Eight Alabama Clergymen." April 12 (1963): Accessed March 28, 2019. https://swap.stanford.edu/20141218230016/http://mlk-kpp01.stanford.edu/kingweb/popular_requests/frequentdocs/clergy.pdf.
10 King, *Why We Can't Wait*, 81.
11 Ibid., 86.
12 For an account of King's response to the clergyman's critique and the way his letter took shape, see Branch, *Pillar of Fire*, Part 1.
13 X & Haley, *Autobiography of Malcolm X*, 36, 271.
14 King, *A Testament of Hope*, 219.
15 Peterson, *Seeds of the Kingdom*, 140.

16 This was one of the ways Malcolm X distinguished himself from King, and it cannot be a coincidence that the first chapter of the former's autobiography was entitled "Nightmare."

17 See especially Harding, *Martin Luther King, the Inconvenient Hero* and Cone, *Martin & Malcolm & America.*

18 King, *Testament of Hope*, 257.

19 King, *Strength to Love*, 83.

20 Ibid., 82.

21 Alexander, *New Jim Crow*, 21.

22 King, *Testament of Hope*, 344–345.

23 Ibid., 48.

24 See King, *Stride Toward Freedom*, 99. Harvard Sitkoff suggests that King's insistence that activists be aware of the temptation toward evil came in part from his personal struggles with his own adultery. (See Sitkoff, *King*, 129ff.)

25 Quoted in Franklin, "An Ethic of Hope," 2.

26 Gandhi, *Autobiography.*

27 Of course, King's awareness of human limitations also came from his own failings, most famously exemplified in his adulterous affairs and his plagiarism in academic and other writings. See especially Sitkoff, *King.*

28 Burrow, *Extremist for Love*, 248.

29 See, e.g., King, *Testament of Hope*, 13, 52, 252.

30 Brown, *Plan B 3.0*, xiii.

31 King also offers a potential corrective to Al Gore and Stephen Hawking's trust in technological solutions discussed in Chapter 1. In his final book he lamented "the gulf between our scientific progress and our moral progress," observing "a poverty of the spirit which stands in glaring contrast to our scientific and technological abundance. The richer we have become materially, the poorer we have become morally and spiritually." King, *Where Do We Go From Here*, 171.

32 King was also informed by the existential theology of Paul Tillich (see especially *Dynamics of Faith*). However, recent scholarship has emphasized the moral and historical importance of noticing the ways his church shaped him long before and much more deeply than the theologians of European descent he studied in school. See especially Baldwin, *There is a Balm in Gilead* and Cone, *Martin & Malcolm & America.*

33 See especially Moe-Lobeda, *Resisting Structural Evil.*

34 Naomi Klein, "Capitalism vs. The Climate." *The Nation*, November 9 (2011): Accessed February 19, 2013, http://www.thenation.com/article/164497/capitalism-vs-climate#.

35 For the full articulation of Klein's position, see *This Changes Everything.*

36 Of course, King's own leadership did not always demonstrate all these traits, which proves the difficulty of achieving King's dream of participatory justice but does not discredit it. The ambiguity created by King's limitations is evidence of, not against, the precarious hope he taught.

37 X & Haley, *Autobiography of Malcolm X*, 274.

38 In an interview, he described his conversion this way: "Mr. [Elijah] Muhammad came along with his religious gospel and introduced the religion of Islam and showed the honesty of Islam, showed the justice of Islam, the freedom in Islam. Why naturally, just comparing the two, Christianity had already eliminated itself, so all I had to do was accept the religion of Islam." (Clark, *The Negro Protest*, 22.) Louis DeCaro notes that, while Malcolm remembered his father as a Baptist minister, this was not true, and while his parents were Christians, his mother in particular emphasized a diverse religious sensibility that prepared the way for her son's conversion. (DeCaro, *Malcolm and the Cross*, Ch. 5.)

39 X & Breitman, *By Any Means Necessary*, 41.

40 Halberstam, *Queer Art of Failure*.

41 X & Haley, *Autobiography of Malcolm X*, 382.

42 X & Breitman, *Malcolm X Speaks*, 60.

43 Elmessiri, "Islam as a Pastoral in the Life of Malcolm X," in Clarke, *Malcolm X*, 69, 75. Elmesseri also argues that this view of Islam was, ultimately, a "pastoral ideal" abstracted from the realities of the Muslim societies and "the seamy side of the Islamic-Arabic world."

44 X & Haley, *Autobiography of Malcolm X*, 304, 306.

45 X & Breitman, *Malcolm X Speaks*, 196.

46 X explains his name in his autobiography, X & Haley, *Autobiography of Malcolm X*, 199.

47 Michael Eric Dyson finds in this move a symbol of a pattern in X's life: "constant reinvention and self-reconstruction," a steady process of defining one's self in resistance to a system that seeks to dismiss one's personhood. (Dyson, *Open Mike*, 343.) Interestingly, Martin Luther King, Jr.'s father also offers an example of this tradition of renaming and reinvention. He was born Michael King, and only changed his name, and that of the son who was named after him, after being inspired by the legacy of the reformer on a trip to Germany when his son was five years old. See Baldwin, 101–102.

48 X & Breitman, *Malcolm X Speaks*, 118–119.

49 Terrill, "Judgment and Critique in the Rhetoric of Malcolm X," 125.

50 Terrill, "Protest, Prophecy, and Prudence in the Rhetoric of Malcolm X," 26.

51 Consider these words from a speech X gave in Paris: "For a long time, we, the oppressed people, not only in America but in Africa, Asia and elsewhere, had to use someone else's yardstick. When they said 'fast,' what was 'fast' to them was 'fast' to us, but nowadays the yardstick has changed. We got our own yardstick. And when you say a long time this assimilation, or a long time this solution, the thing you don't realize is that other generations used a different yardstick." (X & Breitman, *By Any Means Necessary*, 119.)

52 X & Perry, *Malcolm X*. Using this quote, critical race theorist Reiland Baraka argues that X's thought "provides us with a paradigm of the possibilities of an engaged African-centered radical politics and social theory—a 'critical theory,' if you will" in Rabaka, "Malcolm X and/as Critical Theory," 146.

53 The organization explains its name on a webpage entitled, "The Science," which cites James Hansen as an authority. ("The Science." Accessed August 19, 2014, http://350.org/about/science/.) The classic article by Hansen and colleagues uses paleoclimatological analysis and models of future climate changes to argue that anything over 350 ppm is "too high to maintain the climate to which humanity, wildlife, and the rest of the biosphere are adapted." With characteristic caution, they note that this target should be adjusted "as scientific understanding and empirical evidence of climate effects accumulate." (Hansen, et al., "Target Atmospheric CO_2.")

54 Hansen, et al., "Assessing 'Dangerous Climate Change'."

55 Adam Welz, "Emotional Scenes at Copenhagen." (2009): Accessed December 1, 2014, https://adamwelz.wordpress.com/2009/12/08/emotional-scenes-at-copenhagen-lumumba-di-aping-africa-civil-society-meeting-8-dec-2009/.

56 IPCC, "Summary for Policymakers."

57 350.org, "Science." Accessed February 27, 2019. https://350.org/science/.

58 Nixon, *Slow Violence and the Environmentalism of the Poor*, 263.

59 Ibid., 280.

60 Hamilton, *Requiem for a Species*, x–xi.

61 X & Breitman, *By Any Means Necessary*, 105.

62 For the most comprehensive discussion of the ways King and X complemented and corrected one another, see Cone, *Martin & Malcolm & America*, Ch. 9.
63 David, *Martin Luther King, Jr., Malcolm X, and the Civil Rights Struggle of the 1950s and 1960s*, 135.
64 X & Breitman, *Malcolm X Speaks*, 51–52.
65 King, *Why We Can't Wait*, 129, 41–42. Consider, along similar lines, the definition of moderation King offered in an interview:

> I think moderation on the one hand can be a vice; I think on the other hand it can be a virtue. If by moderation we mean moving on through this tense period of transition with wide restraint, calm reasonableness, yet militant action, then moderation is a great virtue which all leaders should seek to achieve. But if moderation means slowing up in the move for justice and capitulating to the whims and caprices of the guardians of the deadening status quo, then moderation is a tragic vice which all men of good will must condemn.
>
> (King, *Testament of Hope*, 661)

5

LOVING THE WORLD WITHOUT CERTAINTY

E. O. Wilson loves the natural world. An entomologist by training, a naturalist by disposition, and an environmentalist by allegiance, he has devoted much of his prolific talent and considerable intellect to sharing what he loves about the world and convincing others to treat it lovingly. He writes, "To know this world is to gain proprietary attachment to it. To know it well is to love and take responsibility for it."[1] In 1984, he published *Biophilia*, introducing the thesis that the human species has an innate desire to connect with other forms of life, that it is human nature to love nature. In later works, he has built on this argument to advocate the protection of other species, using the love of nature to advocate environmentalist positions.[2]

Wilson's environmental credentials are impressive, and he is an influential scientist with a gift for communicating broadly. All environmentalists should appreciate what he has accomplished enhancing environmental literacy, education, and advocacy. However, in the context of a book that questions certainties, we do wonder about his certainty that human beings have an innate "love" for the world that should be nurtured, or that recognizing such love will somehow "naturally" lead to a way of life that is more ecologically sound. As previous chapters show, we worry that a goal laid out without uncertainties or qualification serves a globalized model of monolithic expansion. The authors of this book fear any call that "we" should "love" "nature" with urgency. In order to love, one must love specific things, and when one loves specific things one protects those things, sometimes at the cost of others. In other words, it is easy to fall into an efficient model of what good (protecting those things we love) and bad (fighting against those things that threaten our loves) might mean. When we do that, we operate at the pace of progress rather than ambiguity.

We will not argue against love, nor against love for the natural world. But we do want to think considerably more about what these terms mean and how they influence human behavior. What does it mean to love all of life? What are the implications of such love, the limitations, and the exclusions implied by such love? Learning from Christian ethicist Margaret Farley, we wonder about the dangers of a bad and mistaken love for nature as well as the advantages of a healthy love. She writes in her book on sexual ethics, "There are wise loves and foolish, good loves and bad, true loves and mistaken loves. The question, ultimately, is, what is a right love, a good, just, and true love?"[3] However, in the context of an ethics based upon uncertainty and unknowing, we are less comfortable than Farley with the ideas of unqualifiedly "good" or "true" love. So the goal of this chapter is a better love, a more true love for the world.

In *Becoming Animal*, philosopher David Abrams helpfully describes love's "gravitational draw":

> This gravitational draw that holds us to the ground was once known as Eros—as Desire!—the lovelorn yearning of our body for the larger Body of the Earth, and of the earth for us. The old affinity between gravity and desire remains evident, perhaps, when we say that we have *fallen* in love—as though we were off-balance and tumbling through air, as though it was the steady pull of the planet that somehow lay behind the eros we feel toward another person.[4]

At its most basic level, love is attraction between things, subjects, places, and events. But within that basic idea of attraction is a great deal of ambiguity. The English word to "love" someone includes the attraction a spouse feels for her partner, a parent for his child, a sibling for their sister, a cat-owner for his pet, a man for his favorite shirt, and a person for a welcome beverage. We feel an attraction to each thing, we "love" them, but such "love" is very different in each case.

Given this ambiguity, how could the attraction between human beings and life be better and more true than it currently is? We will engage that question in three steps. First, what is the object of love? What is it that is loved, what is the scale and scope of love's object? Can we love the global when we experience love in its particularities? Can a local and particular love ever make a global difference? Second, what does it mean to love? How much do we need to understand "nature" in order to love it? How much would it need to understand us? Could we love the world and still seek some mastery over it, still extract resources for our needs or wants? Third, who is it that loves? Is "loving the world" elitist, is it sensible only for privileged peoples whose basic needs and immediate families are taken care of? Is it anthropocentric, inflicting a human emotion upon the nonhuman world?

This chapter will not finally answer these questions. The great freedom of a book about unknowing is how many questions we can admit we will not resolve. But we are confident that considering these issues will lead toward a more constructive love, whatever love might be, whoever might be doing it, and whatever it is they might be loving.

What are we loving when we love the world?

The 1968 Apollo mission took a photo of the Earth from space, the "blue marble," that became a rallying point for the emerging U.S. environmental movement of the early 1970s. The idea that all history, all wars, all inventions, all knowledge, all religions, all art, and all cultures were together on one tiny planet seen from the outside changed the way some human beings thought about the earth and our place within it. This was a vital contribution to the growth of environmentalism: people had a picture to symbolize the moral claim that we rise and fall together as a planetary community on this one blue planet spinning in and through space. When E. O. Wilson advises people to love "the world," this is likely what many in his audience picture.

However, a photograph of the earth from space is, inevitably, an abstraction, something that can only be seen, and therefore only loved, from some distance. The strength of this picture is also its weakness: it zooms out so far from human experience that every life on earth, every culture, every species, is unified. The earth becomes an individual. This is helpful because we can love an individual planet as we love our partners, our friends, our family members, our dogs. But the risk of individuality is the perception of indivisibility; the diversities and tensions all across the planet are hidden when it is understood as a single object.

Responding to these limitations of a view of the planet from space, some environmentalists advocate not love for "the world" but for particular places, emphasizing specificity rather than globality. Gary Snyder, a Zen Buddhist and influential bioregionalist, insists, "It is not enough to just 'love nature' or to want to 'be in harmony with Gaia.' Our relation to the natural world takes place in a place, and it must be grounded in information and experience."[5] Snyder has committed himself to his bioregional home of Northern California, which he calls Shasta, and emphasizes that his environmentalism is about aligning to this place, knowing its rhythms, and committing his life to it as it gives him life. Loving the concrete hills and valleys of one's immediate surroundings is very different from loving "the world," and offers a contrasting approach to environmentalism.

Of course bioregionalism, too, is limited. In her book, *Apocalypse Now and Then*, Catherine Keller warns about the violence that can occur when love of place is separated from the broader time and relationality that shape that place.[6] Just as the love one feels for one's family can be warped into a hateful feud against others, so our love affair with a region can become a way to wall our own place off from its surroundings and protect it at all costs. When allegiance to a particular place becomes a "Not In My Backyard" attitude that externalizes threats onto others, it is yet another way of conscripting "nature" into the efficiency of a global capitalism in which everything is placed in a value hierarchy. We can begin to focus so much on a place—that family farm, that creek where I used to look for crawdads, that mountain I like to climb, or that beach where I surf—that we miss our relationships to other places. What about the waste created by our travel to these specific locales? What about the funds diverted to protect these places while others are ignored? And as climates and bioregions begin to shift, what will we do to protect and preserve that which we love in the face of its inevitable change?

Take, for example, the formation of national parks and preserves. These are usually hailed as important conservationist moves that help to create spaces where people can get out "into nature." But their creation has often involved the removal of local/indigenous peoples from the land in order to create a place where others can retreat. The very creation of "natural" places that people have come to love and identify comes at cost for others. The ability to enjoy such places is, all too often, an expression of socio-economic privilege. How does the maintenance of national parks and preserves divert time and resources toward certain experiences of loving nature vs. others? Along these lines, Rob Nixon points out that tourists' "safari" experiences on the African continent express ideas strikingly resonant with colonial understandings of "nature."[7]

Both the global and bioregional approaches seek to love a concrete thing—either the earth as a whole or a particular place on it. Both are made possible by the *reality* of what is loved. We can love the world because we can see a picture of the whole thing; we can love a bioregion because we can map the course of its rivers and feel its dirt between our toes. Love has an object.

But in an ethics of unknowing, de-emphasizing certainties, perhaps environmentalists should learn to love something less concrete, less real, less proven? Upon what could a multiscalar, uncertain love possibly focus?

Ursula Heise offers a helpful proposal, suggesting that 21st century environmentalism should use an image like Google Earth: one can see the whole, but also focus in on all of the different textures and contours of the planet and see how these different places are divided and connected. Rather than representing a singular and "natural" world, this Google Earth image acknowledges that any "world" we understand has been shaped and conditioned by multiplicities of technology, humanity, and the nonhuman, combining to create a multitudinous and evolving understanding.[8] To love this object is to love our best-but-necessarily-partial construction of what is real.

There is, of course, some irony to calling on Google Earth as a moral tool while developing an ethic in opposition to corporate globalization and capitalism. Google is a for-profit enterprise, and its investors have made a fortune through technologies that expanded industrial activity and consumed considerable resources. We admit this irony, and noting it helps us to reiterate an assumption of the book: there is no pure moral stance, no objective space of removal. In a world defined by corporations and globalization, one cannot characterize the environment entirely distinct from these forces. We are always locked into specific histories, biologies, times, and places. We do not mean to endorse Google, but rather to understand and use it as a force currently shaping the world, our understanding of it, and our ability to imagine loving it. This is another way that Google Earth might help us to recognize the fragmented nature of love.

To love the "world" captured by Google Earth is not to embrace global or bioregional thinking, nor to seek a middle ground between them. It is simultaneously more and less than either option. Google Earth depicts something bigger than any region and inherently reminds us that we all always depend on networks that reach across the planet. Google Earth is more obviously relational than the detached image of the blue ball spinning in space, it reminds us of the vast diversities and differences within and between any landscape, any spot on earth.

Google Earth is also far less personal than either the globe or the bioregion. To love Google Earth is to very explicitly and self-consciously love an abstraction. We cannot see Google Earth without realizing that what we love is mitigated and flattened by a screen. We cannot interact with Google Earth without realizing that we are using the clumsy tools of a keyboard, mouse, or touchscreen to extract data from a simulacrum. We learn to love a representation of the world in this image. The world is beyond our understanding, and so loving it is complicated. To love Google Earth is not to love the true world, but it is, perhaps, more true than the picture of Earth from space or a story we might tell ourselves about our bioregion.

Love, knowledge, and unknowing

Margaret Farley argues that a central action of "just, right, and good" love is that it responds authentically to the object. Love should be "a true response to the reality of the beloved, a genuine union between the one who loves and the one loved, and an accurate and adequate affective affirmation of the beloved." Farley's work is on sexual ethics, and so she sums up this claim by saying that love only makes sense when we realize "that *things* are not to be loved as if they were *persons*, and *persons* are not to be loved as if they were *things*."[9]

We will engage two questions about this definition of love. First, Farley's final sentence suggests that there is a difference between loving "things" and loving "people." Does that difference apply to the love of the natural world? Second, Farley suggests that love is always about knowledge: To love another is to know them in their reality, to know them well enough to join them and affirm them. What does it mean to "know" the natural world? We will deal with these questions in turn.

We worry about separating the love of "things" from the love of "people." This is a dangerous worry to raise, because the distinction is generally made to protect vulnerable human beings. We know, for example, that it is problematic when we treat workers like machines, either in the ways we interact with people in daily life or the ways we build and run factories. We know, furthermore, how dangerous it is when we linguistically relate marginalized people to animals and thereby dehumanize them, such as the hurtful dismissal of women implied by the epithet "bitch," which implies that females and dogs are somehow less than men and humans. Critical environmental justice scholar David Pellow names this the "racial discourse of animality," which reveals a troubling intersection between social injustices and attitudes dismissive of the nonhuman world. He suggests that such images are racist and oppressive dismissals of humans and also speciesist dismissals of the other-than-human world.[10] Perhaps the solution is to refuse to treat things poorly, or to refuse to reduce dogs to "things"? In other words, perhaps unjust love is not when a person is treated like a thing, but when any creature or thing is treated cruelly.

The gay community has modeled such thinking by reclaiming animal names. One might be a bear, an otter, a pup, a panda, or a shrimp. All of these describe something that is to be honored within the person; it helps to describe their particular qualities (both in their erotic life and beyond) in ways that lift up a spe-cific animal as a badge of honor. Such animal connections in some cases also allow the person to attempt to empathize with a given type of animal (as is the case with pup–master relationships). Perhaps expressions beyond the queer community—"sly as a fox," "stubborn as a mule," "cougar"—might also be reclaimed in a positive light, not denigrating the human being described but rather com-plementing the non-human species involved in the comparison. Reclaiming human–animal connections in a positive light is one way of blurring the lines between love for humans and the rest of the natural world. This is one way that we can also acknowledge a multiperspectivalism, because if the world is more complicated than the human species, our love for it must be as well.

We should not learn to love all creatures by treating them as "people" or "persons." They are not. Colonization and globalization are caused, in part, by assuming that others are just like ourselves. Europeans justified colonization by convincing themselves that other people wanted "civilization" just like theirs. Capitalists justify economic expansion by convincing themselves that other people want "development" just like theirs. Climate change, a product of colonization and global capitalism, is caused primarily by people who assume that the rest of the world is somehow just like ourselves and will follow the rules we have imagined for our own convenience. We will not save other creatures by bringing them into our species. Such anthropomorphism is a form of domination and control. Other creatures are not human beings, and should not be loved as human beings. They should instead, be loved as themselves.

To love is to change based on what one loves. If each object of love is different, then each love is unique. In part, this returns to the point about scale made in the previous section: to love "the Earth" cannot mean the same thing as loving the woods where I learned to hunt, and neither is it the same as loving the multiscalar simulated world of Google Earth. The first is an abstract and encompassing love. The second is very particular and necessarily exclusive. The third is in constant and complex negotiation. These are different loves because they have different objects.

Such change is continual, because what one loves will, itself, change. No romantic partnership lasts unless it accommodates the ways people involved develop, grow, and struggle over time. Similarly, to love "the world" means loving something constantly in flux, a planet that has developed over four billion years, covered with life that evolved over two billion years and human civilizations that grew over millennia and are now changing the climate and the landscape in rapid and unpredictable ways. We advocate the image of Google Earth as an object for love because it works against simplistic nostalgia for a static image of earth or of home. The images on our screen are inherently fluid, changing over time, mapping the evolving world around us.

Love must change, and any assertion of certainty about love or the object of love denies the possibility of such change. This is in part the critique Whitney Bauman has elsewhere offered of "the monogamy of place": perhaps mono-gamous love is not what is called for in terms of the world, rather what we need is polyamory of places and entities, none of which can be loved in quite the same way.[11] Again, there is something to be learned from queer theory and queer identities: whatever love is, it cannot be contained in the bounds of the hetero-patriarchal monogamous nuclear family, nor within the bounds of human–human love. In fact, very few in human history have lived up to such an ideal (whether "straight", "gay", "lesbian", or "other"). Queer theory's refusal to conclusively define love, identities, or the self says something about the ambiguous and open nature of the erotic connections we make with planetary others (human and non).

This leads to the second question raised above: how do we know what we love? Farley asserts that love is about knowledge, that love requires and assumes a knowledge of the other. E. O. Wilson seems to agree, because he urges people to love the natural world by increasing their knowledge of it. As a sci-entist dedicated to communicating scientific understanding about the world, he is convinced that the more people understand nature the more they will love it. He also suggests that the more we love nature the more we will seek to understand it, making repeated calls for expanded investment in taxonomy, scientific research, and environmental education. Love, for Wilson as well as Farley, is about knowledge, understanding what is loved.

However, Wilson sometimes dangerously equates knowledge with science, leaving little room for other forms of knowing. His 1998 book *Consilience* worked toward a unification of all knowledge based upon a scientific foundation. His 2014 *The Meaning of Human Existence* continued that effort, exploring human nature with a primarily evolutionary lens.[12] The limitations of this perspective are effec-tively pointed out by ethicist Lisa Sideris, who observes that "*science* is not the same thing as *nature*, and to study the former is not to experience the latter." She worries that Wilson and others like him make science "a sacred new mythology" when they suggest that scientific knowledge of the world is a sufficient knowledge of the world.[13] Interested in the emotional wonder of people like Rachel Carson and the experiential knowledge of religious communities, Sideris insists that there is more to knowledge than science.

This means that there is more to loving the world than studying it, which should come as no surprise. A love that simply chronicles, charts, and enumerates the other is, at best, an immature crush. To love the world in a mature way is to seek to know it in many ways, to explore its richness experientially, philosophi-cally, culturally, and physically as well as scientifically. It doesn't require science to tell us that animal–human relations are essential to human happiness, or that a companion animal's happiness is tied to its human partner. Evolutionary biology can tell us that our species has developed along with these creatures, but no one who loves her dog needs a biologist to tell her that she is mentally, imaginatively and psychologically connected to another species. Science can offer a lot of infor-mation about what we are seeing when we look up at the night sky, but it doesn't necessarily give us the sense of wonder or awe that comes from gazing at stars. To know and love Google Earth is not merely to understand it as a technical accom-plishment uniting satellite imagery and complex processers and high-speed connections. It is also to experience the wonder of looking at the same place from multiple angles and at multiple scales, watching the interplay of colors and light on a landscape, and talking about what it means (and its limitations) with others.

In Chapter 2, we discussed the dedication of Marjory Stoneman Douglas to the creation of what we now know as the Everglades. Though her entire life's work was in many ways devoted to the ecological balance between Miami and the Everglades, she was not limited to this place, and so her love was not narrowly bioregional. It was, instead, multiscalar. She loved Florida's cities and its nonhuman landscapes, and she understood how both connected to global systems. She "knew" the world through careful scientific study but also through detailed study of native cultures, personal experiences of places, and ongoing personal interactions with other creatures and people. To ponder what it means to love the world, we might ask "WWMD" (What Would Marjorie Do)?

A love inspired by Douglas could not be static. The ecology of South Florida has always been in flux, and its rate of change is only increasing as the climate changes. Its beaches already flood on certain high tides, fresh water aquifers are already being threatened by the salinization caused by rising sea levels, and the flow of the Everglades from Okeechobee down to the Keys is today possible only because of human engineering. The Everglades may disappear, and a mature love for them would need to consider this possibility and weigh the costs of resisting it against the costs of relocating peoples and cataloging species while it is still possible.

If love incorporates change, it also incorporates an awareness that what we love—at least in this life—will not last forever. So, a genuine love of the Everglades calls for the ability to mourn the loss of a unique but increasingly moribund ecosystem. This will be a challenge, as industrialized peoples in the United States are poorly prepared to deal with death. A disproportionate amount of money spent on health care goes to the last few months of life, regardless of the quality of that life. We are not good at letting go of people we love. Similarly, we have few tools to let go of ecosystems and bioregions we love. To "hold on" to or, as Bruno Latour suggests, to "Freeze Frame" the worlds in which we live is to seek to possess or incorporate, rather than to love.[14] Just as one can try to "hold on" to the end of a life using every means necessary to ensure just one more day of survival, so too might we do with specific places. But hospice suggests an alternative way of loving someone into death that allows them to live through the process while also coming to terms with it. Ideally, this process helps those who continue to live to deal with the loss of a loved one in a way that re-engages the world.

To love the Everglades raises questions about the ethical efficacy of action. We all know that it feels pleasurable to do something for someone you love, and the same is true for environmentally oriented actions. A count of bird species in the marsh, an educational campaign, and a political protest demanding more funding for national parks all feel satisfying. But if it is likely that the Everglades will disappear, then at some point these actions become expensive and unnecessary life support for a dying patient, and the most important thing to do could be to let go. We hope that point has not yet been reached in this particular ecosystem, we hope that there remain good reasons to do all we can to protect the Everglades, as Marjory Stoneman Douglas did. We hope so. But we cannot be sure that is where we are until we have genuinely considered the alternative, that it could be time for hospice, time to mourn.

To love the world is to seek to know it in all its wild diversity. As anyone who has loved anything knows, this is impossible. And yet it is well worth the effort.

An irreverent lover in a diverse world

The third set of questions for this chapter is about the actor: who is it that loves the world? The model of "loving nature" has to a large extent been based upon the understandings of a universalizable human, an idealized person who develops a feeling toward the rest of the natural world. This model still participates in the very separation and dominion that it seeks to overcome. Such a phenomenological model of knowing, loving, and understanding nature too often mistakes a historically and biologically constructed experience of nature with some sort of metaphysical or ultimate understanding of nature. In other words, it does not adequately place human experiences within a cultural and ecological context.

The most simplistic ideal of loving nature tends to depend upon two separations. First, the human being who loves is too often assumed to be distinctly privileged, a white-skinned and European-related male of means. Second, the human being who loves is distinctly unnatural, not himself a part of nature. The one who loves is separated out from most of humanity and most of the world. An ethic based upon unknowing cannot abide such clean distinctions, and so must find a way to characterize the lover in a broader sense, a human being who is open to and humbly aware of the diversity of her own species and fully a part of the wild diversity of the world.

Twenty-first century environmentalism is working to learn how to embrace the diversity of humanity. In its early incarnations, the movement too often emphasized the moral importance of other species and ecosystems while ignoring the moral importance of human communities. Environmentalism became known for its love of whales and rainforests, but not for its love of the human cultures that coexist with both, much less urban peoples who were too often ignored because of an anti-city bias. Environmentalism was never as misanthropic as its worst critics suggested, and it has come a long way, but it nevertheless remains a part of a culture that privileges certain bodies and certain ideas and excludes others.

"Loving the world" is useless if it is the sole provenance of wealthy and white people. This idea must have some meaning for a more diverse humanity. Fortunately, attention in this direction is expanding in promising ways, particularly as industrialized and western environmentalists learn from our neighbors across the planet.

Take, for example, the archipelago of Indonesia. Indonesia has a very different way of understanding human–earth relations than what the authors of this book learned growing up in the United States. Indonesia never passed through a period in which humans were "removed" from the rest of the natural world. This is clear in its architecture, for instance, which does not seal the inside of buildings and homes off from the rest of the natural world. It is also apparent in the ways that Indonesians themselves inhabit the archipelago while recognizing their own limitations. Indonesia is in the "ring of fire," prone to earthquakes, volcanic eruptions, tsunamis, and cyclones. The archipelago's very ground is always shifting in ways that remind humans they are a part of it rather than in control of it. For this reason, some have argued that human–earth relations in Indonesia might best be understood through the lens of "disaster studies."

The rampant deforestation, coral destruction, and pollution problems of Indonesia will not be solved by arguing for some type of preservation or conservation of a "nature" that is separate from humans. Instead, native Indonesians seek subsistence in a changing world. Fishing villages realize that the rehabilitation of coral reefs is intertwined with their livelihoods. The conversion of the Sumatran rainforest for palm oil production might be mitigated through projects that pay localities to protect forest for other species, such as orangutans, or through increased forest tourism rather than arguing that humans should leave the forest alone all together.

Indonesia is but one example of the many and wildly different ways in which human beings live. The diversity of the human species is vitally important on its own, and it is also important as an expression of the wild diversity in which human beings participate. This world beyond humanity is often quickly explained as "nature," which of course is a social construction. The idea of "nature" did not exist until human beings invented it, so in a very real sense nature does not exist by itself. Even if we defend the idea of nature as a pristine ecosystem without human impacts, no human has ever experienced this—once we experience a place, it is no longer "natural." We may want to appeal to an idea of nature as a system relatively unimpacted by industrial technologies, but after a century of climate change not even that nature exists anywhere on the face of the earth.

However, nature inside our minds is a powerful thing. Indeed, it has reshaped the world. Steven Vogel goes so far as suggesting that "the view of nature as something that needs to be protected because of its independence from human beings may itself be a central part of the environmental problem we face today."[15] The paternalistic idea that human beings should care for a nature separate from ourselves led to the kind of careless domination that changes the climate and destroys habitats. Vogel points out that this not only harmed the natural world, but also created a false sense of control—by dismissing some of the world as "natural," we deluded ourselves into thinking that the rest was domesticated. It is not. While all environments have been influenced by human activities, all remain in a very real sense "wild," because no system or structure is ever fully in human control. This is even true of the artifacts we build and our own bodies, which contain wild elements beyond our control. We are each a part of the world and utterly subject to the wildness of that world. So, the one who loves the world must be fully immersed in and subject to it.

Such immersion in the world is religious. Vogel suggests this, insisting that a world without "nature" is also a world without "God," because both appeal to an imaginary "something beyond us or above us to whose dictates we must submit unquestioningly."[16] Vogel takes a stance against what we would call reverence, an attitude to submission and obsequiousness that precludes doubt or self-direction. We might say, then, that loving the world in a postnatural context requires loving the world irreverently.

However, we would disagree with Vogel insofar as he suggests that the idea of "God" always implies reverence in the sense of unquestioning obedience. God is not so easily dismissed or reduced. For example, it is true that the ten commandments in the Hebrew Bible emphasize reverence. The creator is declared "a jealous God" who "will not acquit anyone who misuses his name." But in the narrative these commandments are given to a people who have just been freed from slavery in Egypt, where they had been commanded to worship Pharaoh. Reverence for the Hebrew God meant irreverence toward worldly authority. Jesus continued this Jewish tradition of irreverence in his time: he used the name of God to encourage his followers to leave their families, to pick grain on the Sabbath, to dine with prostitutes, and to consider how rules could serve human beings rather than the other way around. Jesus was then put to death by the Roman Empire, a political authority concerned that he did not sufficiently revere it. In a way, Jesus can be understood as practicing what Jack Halberstam calls "the queer art of failure" discussed in Chapter 2. To love irreverently means to fail to love in the ways set forth by the pace and order of progress. It means to get dirty, messy, and to try out different ways of loving that have not been previously proscribed. It means to break out of idolatries wherever we might find them and connect in new ways with the planetary community around us.

A religious tradition common across many cultures suggests that any God who can be named and understood is a false idol. No human idea is worthy of reverence. The *neti-neti* tradition discussed in Chapter 1 is one example of such thinking. Another is the common Jewish refusal to speak the Hebrew name of God. Still another is the apophatic tradition of Christian theology, exemplified by the early theologian Cyril of Jerusalem's statement that "in what concerns God to confess our ignorance is the best knowledge." To revere God, in all these traditions, is to irreverently question any human idea of God.

If environmentalists seek to love the world, we must similarly question any human idea of the world. Simplistic explanations of "nature" deserve irreverence. Privileged assumptions that any one human community can speak for the entire species deserve irreverence. Confidently pessimistic predictions about what is "inevitable" in global politics deserve irreverence. So, for that matter, do confidently optimistic predictions. To revere the world means being irreverent about oversimplifications of it.

Revering the world at the pace of ambiguity means loving what is unknown rather than what is known. To confidently believe that we know enough to love the world, a place, or a person, is a profound mistake. We must, instead, love out of our ignorance. We must admit how little we understand about the diversity of humanity, and we must continue learning about love from marginalized and silenced human communities. We must admit how little we understand about the world of which we are a part, and love from the mysteries within it.

Love of the unknown

E. O. Wilson is right that environmentalism should nurture love for the world. But this is the beginning of a long and complicated conversation. To love the world is to love a reality in which we are entirely immersed, which we can never fully understand. To love the world in a time of climate change is to love a flux.

We have argued here that loving nature means refusing to revere anything less than the wild diversity of the systems in which we participate, and the best symbol for these systems that we have found is Google Earth. This is love at the pace of ambiguity because it seeks knowledge without expecting to fully know. Indeed, it assumes that we will always have impartial knowledge, and that the truest love we can manage is for a simulation. We have much to learn from that simulation, but it will never explain all of reality. This is an ethics of unknowing. It may be uncomfortable to admit that we cannot know even what we love. But, as the next chapter will show, the hubris of assuming one understands the object of love does real, concrete damage.

Notes

1 Wilson, *Future of Life*, 131.
2 Wilson, *Biophilia*. For Wilson's fullest account of his own affection for nature, see his *Naturalist*.
3 Farley, *Just Love*, 197.
4 Abram, *Becoming Animal*, 27.
5 Snyder, *Practice of the Wild*, 39.
6 Keller, *Apocalypse Now and Then*, Ch. 4.
7 Nixon, *Slow Violence and the Environmentalism of the Poor.*
8 Heise, "From the Blue Planet to Google Earth."
9 Farley, *Just Love*, 198. Emphasis original.
10 Pellow, "Toward a Critical Environmental Justice Studies," 226–227.
11 Bauman, *Religion and Ecology*.
12 Wilson, *Consilience* and *The Meaning of Human Existence*.
13 Sideris, "Science as Sacred Myth?", 147 and 149. See also Sideris, *Consecrating Science*.
14 Latour, "Thou Shalt Not Freeze-Frame or How Not to Misunderstand the Science and Religion Debate."
15 Vogel, *Thinking Like a Mall*, 31.
16 Ibid., 238.

6

THE DANGERS OF BUILDING WITHOUT AMBIGUITY

Spirituality and utopianism in Frank Lloyd Wright

with Richard Bohannon

On the island of Java in Indonesia, most homes in villages, towns and cities are built close together and open to the elements, with wide-open spaces where a large community can gather. In most communities in the U.S., by contrast, homes tend to be built with clear and substantial divisions, hermetically sealing inhabitants from the rest of the world and from neighbors. These are physical manifestations of attitudes about what it means to be human: Javanese religion and philosophy view each person as a self-in-community, and human beings are "archipelagically" linked to one another and to other creatures.[1] In the U.S., most people instead view humanity individualistically, distinguishing themselves from others with a self-contained narrative of a single life from cradle to grave.[2] In both places, architecture reflects deeply held values and beliefs, and trains people to see those values and beliefs as simplistically true. To keep one's home open and to recognize wide-ranging relations to others is simply common sense in a Javanese community of open buildings. To lock the door at night and think of one's life story as a private narrative is common sense in a United States of suburban houses.

The dreams, values, and beliefs of a society are made material in the buildings, streets, machines, and places we construct.[3] The "built" environment tells us a great deal about who we are, because the places and spaces we construct shape understandings of human beings, the ecosystems in which we live, and the other animals and plants with whom we share those ecosystems. It is important, then, for a book about environmental ambiguity to include reflections on the built environment. The previous chapter noted that "loving" nature is a complicated and contested category; this chapter further explores the ways any relationship to anything "natural" is shaped by human artifacts.

Modern urban planning developed between the late 19th and middle 20th centuries in North American and Europe, arriving on the heels of technological change and massive industrialization. Early urban planners, as members of an emerging professional field, worked to avoid some of the basic side-effects of massive urban industrialization—profound air and water pollution, and their incumbent effects on human health—by taking advantage of the industrial age's transportation innovations of trains and automobiles. Fossil-fueled transportation changed what was possible in terms of where people could live within and around cities. Cities like Manchester, England and New York, New York were shaped by industries in their centers that came with pollution and cramped living conditions, but they were also shaped by industrialists who profited from those activities and used the profits to take advantage of growing rail networks to separate their private and home lives from their work and its byproducts.

The product of this outward migration is the suburb, and it remains with us today, especially in the U.S., Canada and Australia. Suburbs moved the homes of the managing class—and then the middle classes, and now often the working class—out of city centers and into the surrounding countryside. Railroads first allowed for bedroom communities to sprout along the peripheries of large cities, huddled around train stations. Then the automobile truly set suburbia and its inhabitants free from the confines of the polluting industrial city and allowed the footprint of cities to sprawl in all directions.

This narrative of surburbanization is, in part, about race and gender. In the U.S., suburbs are a manifestation of the ways white people sought to remove themselves from increasingly diverse communities, maintaining physical and cultural separation even as segregationist policies became illegal. In the 19th century, cities were also viewed suspiciously as places that would "sissify" men, and so suburbs, much like national parks, became a way to escape into nature and also solidify manhood.[4] Part of this manhood involved a physical limitation of women in wealthy households, as men freely moved between city and suburb but women were expected to largely confine themselves to the private, domestic sphere of the suburb.

The narrative of suburbanization is also a *religious* history. Many of the figures who imagined the modern city were influenced by explicit and deeply held convictions, including prominent planners and architects such as Ebenezer Howard, Buckminster Fuller, le Corbusier, and Frank Lloyd Wright, as well as many more experimental designers, such as Paolo Soleri.[5] Their work reflects the religious worldviews they held, and the broad project of suburbanization was often described with religious metaphors of return to some sort of idyllic, Edenic state.[6]

This chapter focuses on Frank Lloyd Wright (1867–1959), who is perhaps the best-known 20th century architect in the United States. Wright was an influential architect and a prolific writer, and his work is relevant to our topic not only because it attempted to bridge between the built and the nonhuman environment, but also because his understanding of "nature" was explicitly religious. Wright will help us further and more concretely explore the potential and pitfalls of what it can mean to reverently love nature.

Highly regarded for his efforts to "return" urban existence to a better relationship with the surrounding natural world, Wright sheds light on the inevitability of complicity and ambiguity, both in the ways his own work wrestled with separations between humanity and nature and in the long-term, unintended consequences of his creations exacerbating such separation. His architectural achievements continue to help people think about the inherent relationship of all human artifacts to the natural world, and yet he also set the stage for late 20th and early 21st century suburban sprawl. Wright is therefore something of a negative object lesson in the need for humility, which he lacked in his professional convictions. Wright questioned the certainty of others' assumptions about architecture (though perhaps not his own), and yet he helped to form the rarely questioned pace of progress in contemporary life.

Unlike the historical figures in previous chapters, we are not writing about Frank Lloyd Wright in order primarily to learn from his wisdom. To the contrary, in this chapter, we hope to learn from Wright's limitations. While he was brilliant and incorporated a deep love for nature into his work, the results have been eco-logically destructive and we believe this is related to the fact that Wright was insufficiently aware of his own limitations and fallibility.

The philosophy and religion of Frank Lloyd Wright

Wright considered himself a spiritual person and grew up in a religious, albeit unorthodox, household. His mother was a Unitarian, the daughter of a Uni-tarian minister from Wales. His father was originally a Baptist preacher, but converted to Unitarianism and brought a plurality of religious voices to Wright's childhood. As one author notes, after his conversion Wright's father "stopped preaching, studied Sanskrit and chanted the mantras and hymns of the Vedic texts to help him understand the divinity present in the cosmos and inner self." In addition, Wright's parents exposed him to transcendentalism, a movement that promoted the inspiration of one's own "inner light."[7]

Transcendentalism was perhaps the dominant spiritual tradition evident in Frank Lloyd Wright's work, and it influenced him throughout his life. Early in his career, he expressed particular familiarity with the works of Walt Whitman and Ralph Waldo Emerson; by the 1930s he frequently quoted Henry David Thoreau as well.[8]

Whitman, Emerson, and Thoreau promote a deep love for nature that comes from quietly listening to the world beyond the human. All three suggest that one needs to learn to hear, see, and think differently in order to love the earth. This is a reverence for the world that is compatible with an ethic of unknowing in that all listening requires openness and uncertainty. Having learned from these ideas, trans-cendentalism, Frank Lloyd Wright worked to make architecture "listen." His designs form a synthesis of a mid-century modernistic aesthetic with a transcen-dentalist perspective, with the modern building as an outcropping of his world-view.[9] "Like Thoreau," Naomi Uechi writes, "Wright also believes that the ultimate goal of simplicity is not to simplify everything but rather to help humans to receive artistic intuition from the divine and from the natural world around them."[10] His work was always functional, but part of a building's function, he believed, was to shape human beings as spiritual and moral beings.

Another lesson Wright adapted from transcendentalism was the importance of patterning his designs after those he found in the natural world. He was particularly fond of a quote from Thoreau's *Walden* about the spots on a tortoise shell, which argues in part that "a man has no more to do with the style of his house than a tortoise with that of its shell."[11] Naomi Uechi notes that Wright called Thoreau's line "the best essay on organic ornament I have ever read," and that he learned from it:

> that ornamentation should be like the tortoise's spotted shell, which is natural, simple, and beautiful because it reflects 'the necessities and character' of the tortoise and is not gaudy like the ornamentation of Trinity Church on Broadway. For Wright, the relationship between humans and architecture is similar to that between a tortoise and its shell because both houses and shells protect living beings from the heat, cold, rain, snow, storms, and wind. Both houses and shells also express living beings' identity; therefore, they reflect 'the necessities and character' of their dwellers.[12]

For Wright, as for the transcendentalists, the modern, mechanistic world was misguided because it separated people from nature. The solution was a more naturalistic idea about what it means to be human in the world. To put it in the language we have used elsewhere in the book, modern technologies of becoming—here architecture and city planning—were creating abjections of humans and the rest of the natural world. Through his new architectural style, Wright sought to listen to those abjections and to re-think human–earth relations.

More than simply a theoretical and literary re-use of Thoreau, Wright attempted a Thoreauvian kind of simplicity and self-sufficiency in his own life. At Taliesin in Wisconsin, which served as both home and studio for himself and several apprentices, he established a kind of laboratory to try out new technologies of becoming. Taliesin was "to be self-sustaining if not self-sufficient and with its domain of two hundred acres, shelter, food, clothes and even entertainment within itself. It had to be its own light-plant, fuel yard, transportation and water system."[13] Architectural residents grew their own food, raised cattle, and constructed a small dam along the edge of the property which created a reservoir reminiscent (perhaps unintentionally) of Walden Pond. The dam also increased Taliesin's self-sufficiency by providing it with its own source of electricity.

Wright was also influenced by theosophical philosophy, a movement that merged European philosophy with ideas taken from Hinduism and Buddhism and teaches that there is a single Absolute in the universe of which everything is an emanation. Influential theosophist Rudolph Steiner, like the transcendentalists, sought to re-think the relationship of divinity and the world (and thereby what it meant to be human). Steiner articulated his philosophy as a correction against both the entrenched dogmatic theism he saw in Christianity and the dogmatic materialism he saw in scientific culture, and he believed that human beings were fulfilled when we enter into harmony with the world by synthesizing our natural, material selves with our spiritual, thinking selves. Eugenia Ellis observes that when Wright opened his own firm in 1898, the insignia he used to sign drawings borrowed a theosophical symbol to signify "divine creation."[14] Inspired by the harmony of the Absolute in Theosophy, Wright worked toward an architectural style that combined and transcended the material and the spiritual, the industrial and "the wild."

Demonstrating how transcendental and theosophist his thinking was, Wright attributed his own ideas as much to experiences of the non-human world as to any philosophical tradition. "Philosophy came to me gradually," he writes, "and mostly by way of experience on the farm, care of animals, etc.—the mysterious beauties and obvious cruelties of Nature. These interlocking interchanges of the universe began to fascinate me more then and were with me when I began to build. It was then that I became a seeker of Truth of Form from the inside out." He continues: "A struggle against nature never appealed to me. The struggle for and with Nature thrilled me and inspired my work."[15]

The religious tenor of Wright's "struggle with and for Nature" is perhaps most clear in a 1957 interview with Mike Wallace, where a 90-year-old Wright insists, "I've always considered myself deeply religious." Wright had moved on somewhat from his Unitarian upbringing, and so when asked if he went to church, he replied, "Yes, I go occasionally to this one and then sometimes to that one, but my church, I put a capital "N" on Nature and go there." To emphasize the point, he interrupted Wallace's next question and remarked, "You spell God with a 'G,' don't you? ... I spell nature with an 'N,' capital."[16] This could be interpreted either as a pantheistic claim that Nature is itself the divine, or a transcendental idea that Nature points to a God beyond and behind it. Perhaps the distinction was unimportant for Wright. It is certain, though, that his religious naturalism helped him to create structures that reworked the ways in which humans interact with the rest of the natural world.

Wright sought Truth and its architectural companion, Form, through encounters and interactions with Nature; all were capitalized ideals, all were basic realities to be discovered and celebrated in the world around him. We find in this a tendency for certainty, the type of uncritical reverence critiqued in the previous chapter and, as discussed below, we believe that this is linked to the emergence of the suburbs. However, Wright's desire to struggle "for and with Nature," to bring apparently rival ideas without choosing between them, is an important nod to complexity, reflected in the "organic agriculture" from which a great deal can be learned.

Organic architecture

Wright's deep reverence for nature coincided with his strongly anti-urban inclinations, leading to what he called "organic" architecture. This approach does not strive to make buildings look *natural*, per se (there are no glazed windows in nature), nor is it organic in the contemporary sense of reducing environmental impacts. For Wright, organic architecture instead focuses on integrating the design of buildings into their site, respecting what he saw as the proper use of materials, and designing buildings using basic principles from within the natural world. In the 19-story Price Tower (1952) in Bartlesville, Oklahoma, for instance, Wright used the branches of trees as a model for an economical system of cantilevered floors, imagining the office tower as a "tree" in the city.[17] Likewise, the roof beams and structural columns inside many buildings were intentionally designed to mimic the form of trees.

Organic architecture goes beyond mimicry, however. Wright sought to create architecture that would shape the people who used it.

> Besides serving definite aims [the building] would express, through its own specific geometry, the essential order of the universe. ...A building was to take possession of its surroundings in order to enhance the beauty of its location, just as a lake, a bluff, or a tree enhance the appearance of a landscape. In Wright's utopia, the beauty of buildings would be a per-manent object lesson of the joy of communion with nature.[18]

In other words, what we see in Wright's architecture is a navigation between humans–technology–nature in which they are all thought of together, with an attempt to let "Nature" lead the way.

Perhaps Wright's best known work is a private residence called Fallingwater, a perfect example of his "organic" architecture. The home is a complex, modernist layering of horizontal and vertical lines, with stone and plaster exterior walls reflecting the rock outcroppings along the creek over which a portion of the house is cantilevered. Trees huddle close by, leaving no room for lawns. The building's name comes from the creek and waterfall that run beside and partially underneath it. As architectural historian Kathryn Smith observes,

> Fallingwater illustrates more clearly perhaps than any of Wright's other waterfall buildings... his effort to forge a spiritual unity between architecture and nature. ...While the building differentiates itself from its surroundings and retains its identity as a man-made object, it is perceived as a complement to nature, and, as a result, each ennobles the other by its presence.[19]

Such a "spiritual unity," for Wright, is not found in a simple "return" to nature from modernity—the architecture is after all the result of modern technology. Nor is he simply turning "nature" into an object for modern projects. Rather, his architecture forges a new, more ambiguous, type of space in which humans, technology, and the rest of the natural world come together.

Organic architecture has influenced successive generations of architects. The U.S. architect Fay Jones, for instance, was a student of Wright's and is known especially for his evocative, light-filled sacred spaces. His Thorncrown and Cooper Memorial chapels, both constructed in northwest Arkansas in the 1980s, were built in midst of forests, whose forms they mimic and whose interior space is very much defined by its ability to embrace and celebrate the exterior world surrounding it.[20]

The concept of organic architecture forms a precursor to modern "green" architecture–though the latter tends to be more concerned with the performance than the aesthetics of the built form. The contemporary Australian architect Glenn Murcutt, who won the 2002 Pritzker Prize,[21] for instance, focuses explicitly on sustainability and describes himself as both "Thoreauvian and Wrightian." Murcott's architecture, unlike Wright's, is primarily concerned with the efficiency of a given component or structure rather than with creating a new, third space that integrates humans, the rest of the natural world, and the built environment. Architectural critics have derided Murcott as "only designing boxes that perform well," something no one would have said about Wright.[22] In other words, Wright sought not to reduce the carbon footprint of a building, but to use a building to teach people to re-think human–nature relations.

Here we think there is something important to learn from Wright. Contemporary environmental architecture, such as represented by the United States Green Building Council's LEED certification program, is resolutely focused on function, measuring the energy use and carbon output of buildings while paying relatively little attention to the experience created by a space and what it teaches people about their relationship to the natural world.[23] Wright's organic agriculture, which largely pre-dates the modern environmental movement, reminds us that every human being's impact on the environment is shaped by spiritual factors—who we believe ourselves to be, how we understand ourselves to be in relationship to one another and the world around us, and what we feel empowered to do.

So, organic architecture is a reminder that the environments we build create "common sense" understandings of the world, communicating to people the ways they are or are not in relationship with the non-human world. If we strive to nurture a multiperspectival, developing love for nature, then Wright has much to teach us about what sorts of spaces make such a love possible, what kinds of structures help to open people to the natural world while also preserving the complexity of every human interaction with the natural world. In this way, Wright is a model to be followed.

Nature and the city: the emergence of the suburban

In another sense, though, Wright was too confident in his own synthesis of the material and spiritual, too certain that he could access "Truth" and "Nature," and here he becomes a more negative example not only in his hubris but also in the physical effects of his work. Wright's belief in an absolute Nature led him to move away from urban centers and into surrounding undeveloped and agricultural areas that he helped to transform into suburbs. Perhaps learning from Thoreau, Wright's reverence for nature was coupled with a disdain for urban life. He designed buildings that organically flowed with the natural world, but he believed that he had to get out of the city to do so. Fallingwater is located 40 miles southwest of Pittsburgh, for instance, constructed in 1935 as a weekend residence for the family of Edgar Kaufmann, Sr., who owned a downtown department store. As the art critic Donald Hoffmann notes, Wright believed that "nature held the moral corrective to the artificial and debased life of the modern city. Measured against nature, cities were dreary, sterile, confused, unhealthy, ugly places."[24]

While he did design a few urban buildings, like the Guggenheim Museum in New York City, it is notable that Wright's only two constructed high-rises—the SC Johnson Wax Research Tower in Racine, WI (1944) and the Price Tower in Bartlesville, Oklahoma (1952)—were built more for a car-oriented suburban office park than a traditional downtown business district. Wright's antipathy toward cities manifested itself not simply in designing rural outposts for wealthy families, but also in the development of modern suburbia. In other words, out of the third space where modernity and nature come together emerged a different kind of place, a place with disastrous environmental impacts.

In the mid-1920s, Wright became increasingly interested in designing utopian communities away from urban centers. Narciso Menocal argues that Wright's work should be identified with the "jeremiad, that quintessentially American dictum that promises utopia to those who embrace nature after stepping out of history and tradition." Like Whitman before him, Wright believed that "Nature" is necessary for democracy to work and that "democracy had not yet been established in the land."[25]

Wright sought to model a utopian democratic community in a built utopia that learned from nature in a development called Broadacre City, aspects of which were also known as Usonia.[26] Broadacre was an idealized, suburban anti-city, a set of ideas he did not expect to be constructed. It was created as a prototype for the perfect city of the future. Transportation was based on automobiles, pedestrianism not accommodated for, and the individual homestead was the City's symbolic center,[27] with each home placed on at least one acre of its own. Unlike filthy industrial cities that required shared parks, Broadacre would provide privately owned green space for every resident, ensuring both their physical and psychological health. Much like Thoreau's blending of a reverence for nature with a strident individualism, Wright's vision of Broadacre was not only about integrating humans with nature, but also about an individualistic ideal of democracy, personal freedom, and cooperative living that resists the tyranny of the state.

Wright designed and built a number of individual houses in what became known as the Usonian style—often low-slung, single story homes—intended as affordable homes for the middle class. While he never had the opportunity to build an entire city, at the end of his career Wright did plan a neighborhood named Usonia in Mount Pleasant, NY, comprised of 47 homes on 100 acres (including 40 acres of preserved woodland). He designed three of the homes himself, while the rest were built in his style by other architects. Homes in Usonia used passive solar heating and lighting, and the entire neighborhood was initially cooperatively owned and developed. Even after problems with banks and legal issues caused homes to revert to private ownership, the community continued to hold in common the 40 acres of woodland surrounding the development.[28]

Suburbia is often caricatured as a bastion of loneliness, but this does not appear to be the case for many residents of Usonia. While the community is now quite affluent, most of the homes were built inexpensively, often using communal help from neighbors. Despite the big lots, the neighbors knew each other well. In a retrospective article in the *New York Times*, one former resident comments that in Usonia she "felt comfortable walking into almost any house in the community... And I grew up calling adults by their first name. It was a very comfortable kind of feeling, people were very accepting of one another. I haven't lived in Usonia for 10 years but I still feel like there are five or six families I could turn to in time of need, with total faith that they would come through for me."[29] Again, such fluidity between inner and outer, between self and other, and between families is one of the intended goals of Wright's organic architecture. He created spaces that changed the ways people relate to one another and to the rest of the natural world.

Still, Usonia, NY, is a suburb. And while a suburb with passive solar and a preserved forest is less environmentally destructive than some neighboring communities, it is far from environmentally benign. Homes in Usonia are far more energy- and resource-intensive than those in the city of New York an hour's commute to the south.[30] The critic James Howard Kunstler convincingly argues that suburban development is "the most destructive development pattern the world has ever seen, and perhaps the greatest misallocation of resources the world has ever known."[31] Suburbs pull investment and energy out of urban centers. Their creation re-shaped many cities to be overwhelmingly car dependent, fractured, and grossly inefficient. They require far more resources to build and maintain per-capita than their downtown counterparts. Most of this destruction is built into the nature of suburbs: low population density, large homes, and privately-owned lots create environmental problems and discourage community, whether or not the homes use passive solar, whether or not there is a preserved forest.

The final chapter of Wright's *Autobiography* argues that, "True Wisdom is no earthly thing" but rather "a spiritual state attained by refraining from selfish competition, imitation or moralizing. And, most of all, by living in love and harmony with Nature"[32] In another passage he describes Broad-acre as "the organic city", where democracy can thrive, because it would offer a

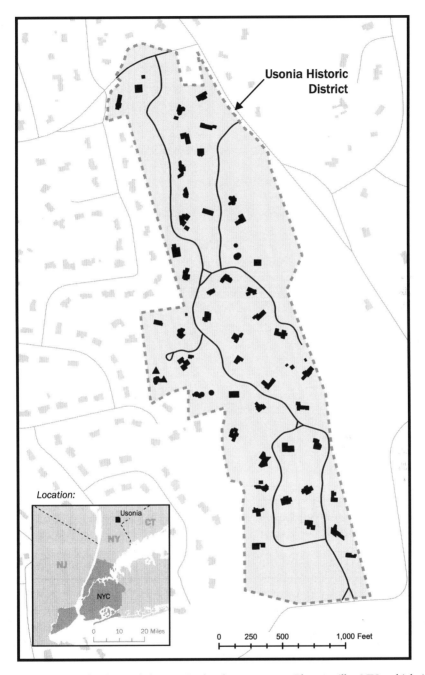

Location:

Usonia Historic
District

Usonia
CT
NY
NJ
NYC

0   10   20 Miles

0   250   500   1,000 Feet

Map 6.1 Frank Lloyd Wright's Usonia development near Pleasantville, NY, which is
        now listed as a National Historic District
Sources: USGS, Westchester County (NY). Map by Richard Bohannon

relaxed, resilient, safe, fundamentally a free, structural form for the life that will, some day, become Usonia, the one great free City so founded in uncommon sense as to make human life not only more beautiful but more secure. More secure and beautiful because more natural to present and future human Life…[33]

This is all predicated on the aforementioned individualism: every family unit should have its own individual houses in the great free City. The desire to have such an individual relationship with nature helped to fuel the flight from city to suburb. As Joseph M. Watson has noted, Wright's anti-urban ideal ignored and exacerbated the racial and economic inequalities that fueled the growth of suburbia in the U.S.[34]

Frank Lloyd Wright helped to create the modern suburb. His organic agriculture contributed substantially to an incredibly inorganic, destructive pattern of development. This is part of his legacy. Of course he did all of his work well before the environmental and social problems of suburbia were widely known, and there was no large-scale environmental movement in his lifetime. We have no interest in blaming him for the environmental impacts of suburbs that he could not have foreseen. We are interested, though, in the ambiguity of his legacy, and in the fact that his certainty, his faith that he could access Nature and Utopia with capital letters, might have prevented him from seeing the limitations of the spaces he was creating. Wright loved the natural world, sought to learn from it, and sought to teach the people who used his buildings to love and learn from nature, too. But he was limited and so the good he could do was limited, too. He was complicit in systems and structures larger than himself and his ideals. So are we all. Thus, 21st century environmentalism must embrace ambiguity, must recognize that even loving N/nature and reverently seeking to live in harmony with it is a slippery goal. Just as the suburb has ended up at least as much a disaster as a utopia, so many of our own actions today will ripple out into unknown effects into the future.

Frank Lloyd Wright's legacy is complicated and cautionary. Understanding his achievement and its limitations reveals that even an ethic based in a deep love and reverence for nature can bring about destructive consequences. This is precisely the recognition Hannah Arendt came to about all actions in the world: we can never know or have any control of our effects once we have acted.[35] So, we must act, assess the effects of actions, and come together again in the polis to renegotiate, or as Latour might argue, to collect ourselves together again.[36]

There are also complications in the legacies of Rachel Carson, Marjory Stoneman Douglas, Martin Luther King, Jr., and Malcolm X. This is true of every single saint, hero, or genius throughout history. Accepting their ambiguity helps us to understand our own so that a) we admit that our heroes had bad ideas as well as good ones; b) we come to recognize the ever-changing nature of what it means to build knowledge and worlds together in a way that challenges anyone's position of certainty; and c) we begin to recognize that multiple perspectives—as messy as they will be—are necessary in order to move into new ways of being in the world that promote the best planetary community possible.

Far more than any of the other figures we have worked with, though, Frank Lloyd Wright believed in certainties, believed that he had access to "Nature with a capital N." This is a problem. Using the ideas developed in the previous chapter, this is a love of the world that is too directed toward a single ideal of what that world is, too singular and therefore too reverent. A more dynamic and uncertain love could have helped him to find beauty in cities as well as outside them, could have helped him to see that the synthesis between the material and the spiritual cannot happen in small subdivisions if the cities and farms between which those subdivisions are built continue to separate people from their environments. Wright shows us the danger of certainty, and so can inspire us to further embrace an uncertain, a dynamic love.

We do not dismiss Wright for his limitations, because we are no more interested in creating a simplistic villain than a simplistic hero. Wright was only one of many progenitors of suburbia, and evidence suggests that he envisioned suburbs more environmentally friendly than they might have been without him. But the ambiguity of this legacy is yet another sign of our insistence on ambiguity in contemporary environmentalism. Utopic orderings of the world can have disastrous consequences if not put into the larger, more complex set of relationships that make up the planetary community.[37]

Loving garbage

In the film *Examined Life*, Philosopher Slavoj Žižek makes the radical claim that a reasonable response to environmental degradation must include a love of garbage. Walking through a dump, he insists that people must "become more artificial" by accepting all the complexities of the world, including the remainders and outcasts of industrial and consumptive lifestyles. The moral life involves finding the "aesthetic dimension, in things like this, in trash itself—that's the true love of the world. Because what is love? Love is not idealization."[38]

Ivone Gebara, an ecofeminist theologian, similarly argues that all theology (and here we might add all ethical deliberation) should be done amidst "garbage and noise."[39] It is amidst the garbage and noise of the urban, the toxic waste site, and the landfill, that the consequences of our policies, ethics, and actions are ultimately fully realized. Dirt, feces, death, and decay are as much a part of our relationship to nature as pristine parks and preserves.[40]

These garbage-, noise-, and waste-loving contributions are important counterbalances to Wright. While the architect revered the natural world and sought to fit his creations within it, his contributions reveal that the world we live in is also filled and defined by unintentional artifacts and cast-offs. We must learn to love those, too. To love the world is to see it as it is, to know that it is messy and broken, to know that parts of it are inevitably dying, and to commit to act on its behalf. Loving the world must mean loving its garbage. Loving a world best represented by Google Earth means loving a world we cannot fully understand, a world we cannot always find lovable, a world we cannot always save.

We love the work of Frank Lloyd Wright as part of the world and part of the legacy of environmentalism. Loving him means seeing both the beauty and the garbage he produced. When he sought to understand "Nature" with a capital "N" as a force to work with and for which he could struggle, Wright captured something powerful. When he neglected the limitations to his own understanding of nature and his work within it, he made a mistake. He did not question the economic and political implications of an ideal, anti-urban development that gives each resident an acre of land and an individualized form of transportation. That this mistake is understandable in Wright's time does not make it anything other than a mistake.

Love is a vital motivation for environmentalism at the pace of ambiguity. But such love must be directed at the real world in all its complexity; it cannot be love for one's self, for a sense of the divine that is a thinly veiled disguise for self-interest, for a romantic ideal of the natural world, or for any human idea that asks for unquestioning reverence. To love the real world is to follow Wright in trying to learn what it means to truly be a part of its organic and inorganic complexity, but also to diverge paths from Wright's legacy and refuse romantic idealizations of nature. To love the real world is to know that, just like Wright, we will make mistakes. Mature love, mature reverence for the world, accepts this and moves ambiguously onward.

Notes

1 On the archipelagic identity, see Boellstorf, *The Gay Archipelago*.
2 Bauman, "Meaning-Making Practices, Copyrights, and Architecture in the Indonesian Archipelago."
3 See, for example, Pierre Bourdieu's discussion on how the physical design of homes in Algerian Kabyle society reinforces gender norms (Bourdieu, *Outline of a Theory of Practice*, 91).
4 See Mortimer-Sandilands & Erickson, *Queer Ecologies*, 1–50.
5 On Howard, le Corbusier and Wright, see Fishman, *Urban Utopias in the Twentieth Century*. Regarding Fuller, see Sieden, *Buckminster Fuller's Universe,* especially pages 88–91. Regarding Soleri, see Soleri, *The Omega Seed*.
6 Merchant, *Reinventing Eden*.
7 Ellis, "The Red Square," 5.
8 Uechi, "Evolving Transcendentalism," 73.
9 As Joseph Connors has explored, Wright was both an heir to the transcendentalist strands of the late 19th century and a witness to the growth of modern technology and machinery and the functionalist architecture that accompanied it; his perspective blended the two. "Wright's thinking was resilient enough to hold both in balance and to explore links between them," Connors writes. "His vision of nature emphasizes its abstract and even mathematical qualities, while his vision of the machine is highly organic and biomorphic." (Connors, "Wright on Nature and the Machine," 2.)
10 Uechi, "Evolving Transcendentalism," 75.
11 Thoreau, *Walden*, 60.
12 Uechi, "Evolving Transcendentalism," 79.
13 Quoted in Ibid., 85.

14 Ellis, "The Red Square," 1. Later in his career, it evolved into a Native American-inspired spiral (12).

15 Wright, *Autobiography*, 594, 597.

16 http://www.youtube.com/watch?v=K9ZHOnmZ7T0, accessed 17 October 2014.

17 See Uechi, *Evolving Transcendentalism in Literature and Architecture*, 158.

18 Menocal, "Sources of Frank Lloyd Wright's Architectural Utopia," 111–112.

19 Smith, "Beat of the Rhythmic Clock of Nature," 229.

20 See Richard R. Bohannon II, "Constructing Nature at a Chapel in the Woods," in Kearns & Keller, *Ecospirit*.

21 The Pritzker is often referred to as the Nobel Prize of architecture. Murcutt and Jones have also both won the American Institute of Architect's (AIA) Gold Medal, the AIA's highest award, in 2009 and 1990, respectively.

22 Uechi, *Evolving Transcendentalism*, 167.

23 See https://new.usgbc.org/leed.

24 Hoffman, "Meeting Nature Face to Face," 90.

25 Menocal, "Sources of Frank Lloyd Wright's Architectural Utopia," 114–116.

26 According to Menocal, "While [Wright] used the term democratic to define utopian behavior, he coined the word Usonian, possibly a combination of U.S. and utopian, to describe the architectural environment of utopia" ("Sources of Frank Lloyd Wright's Architectural Utopia," 113).

27 Fishman, *Urban Utopias*, 157.

28 Elise Brenner, "Green Before It Had a Name," *The New York Times*, April 15, 2007.

29 Quoted in Scott Rilkin, "Usonia Community Remembers Its Past," *The New York Times*, August 30, 1981.

30 See, for instance, Light, "The Urban Blind Spot in Environmental Ethics."

31 James Kunstler, "Remarks in Hudson, NY." Accessed September 5, 2015. http://kunstler.com/other-stuff/speeches-guest-articles/remarks-in-hudson-ny/.

32 Wright, *Autobiography*, 599. Though the chapter's title is "Broadacre City," little energy is spent explaining the buildings or plans themselves.

33 Ibid., 614. Fishman describes this aspect of Broadacre in more detail (*Urban Utopias*, 122ff).

34 Watson, "The Suburbanity of Frank Lloyd Wright's Broadacre City."

35 Arendt, *Human Condition*.

36 Latour, *Politics of Nature*.

37 Keller, *Apocalypse Now and Then*.

38 Taylor et al. *Examined Life*.

39 Gebara, *Longing for Running Water*, 2–3.

40 See also Cohen, *Prismatic Ecology*, 193–212.

7

CONCLUDING IDEAS ON AMBIGUOUS TIME

Discussions of climate change used to be dominated by an argument between those who "believed" and those who "denied" or were "skeptical." The primary question was whether or not climate change was "real." Deniers and skeptics insisted that there was only uncertain or ambiguous evidence for anthropogenic impacts on weather patterns, and environmentalists took the contrary position, insisting that scientists had achieved a consensus, emphasizing the high standards for such a scientific pronouncement, and strongly insisting that the evidence was clear.

Some prominent politicians still deny the reality of climate change, but years of arguing with them has shown environmentalists that it is rarely productive. Most of those who refuse to pay attention to scientific consensus and dismiss truths that conflict with their ideology are trapped in such a narrow view of certainty that there is no rhetoric or argument that will change their minds. They must be worked around, defeated, or converted indirectly through conversations about something other than climate change. Arguing about whether the climate is changing produces nothing but frustration.

Fortunately, the majority of people worldwide have accepted the truth that the climate is changing because of human activity. So, the important question in environmentalist discourse is no longer whether one "believes in" climate change, but rather what should be done about it. Mike Hulme recognizes this and argues that what should be done cannot be "large" or "grand," because it is large and grand thinking that created the problem. He writes:

> If we pursue the route of seeking ever larger and grander solutions to climate change we will continue to end up frustrated and disillusioned: global deals will be stymied, science and economics will remain battlegrounds for rearguard actions, global emissions will continue to rise, vulnerabilities to climate risks will remain. And we will end up unleashing ever more reactionary and dangerous interventions in our despairing search for a solution to our wicked problem: the colonisation of agricultural land with energy crops, the colonisation of space with mirrors, the colonisation of the human spirit with authoritarian government.[1]

We agree, and would add that such large and grand thinking has contributed not just to climate change, but also to so many of the interrelated wicked problems of environmental degradation and globalization that characterize industrialized human life in the 21st century. This has been the argument of our book: certainty colonizes thinking, which leads to colonizing and destructive action.

When debating "is climate change real?", environmentalists had an incentive to take a strong and seemingly certain position. Now that the question has changed to "what should be done about climate change," we must be deeply cautious and suspicious of unequivocal answers. It is time, instead, to stand up against colonization and simplicity with an uncertain ethics at the pace of ambiguity.

As we begin to conclude, we will confess that we are somewhat uncertain about our ethics of uncertainty, concerned with our critiques of environmental concern. While we strongly believe that environmentalism must move forward at the pace of ambiguity, we are aware that the results of our argument will be, at best, ambiguous. The questions that we have heard as we share our ideas with others, the questions we keep asking ourselves, begin with "But what about." We argue for a pace of ambiguity. But what about the glaciers that are already shrinking, closing off water supplies and contributing to sea level rise? We argue for an ethics of uncertainty. But what about the homeless refugees who struggle with uncertainty in the face of unwelcoming and bigoted wealthy communities? We call for love without reverence. But what about the species already driven extinct because industrialized civilization failed to wonder at their unique diversity?

When wicked problems are also immediate problems, it is difficult to treat them with patience. We see the problem and we want to fix it. Our argument is that we must hear the "But what about" questions, but those questions should not lead us to believe that we know what to do. We are learning to accept this, and will conclude our theoretical discussion here by offering a view of time that helps us to do so. This view of time helps us to accept the uneasiness of ambiguity, to attend to the undercommons that requires patience for privileged people to notice, to celebrate that which is un-apocalpytic in our world, and to embrace the universality of imperfection.

The anxiety of chronological time and the bubbling present

Throughout this text, we have focused on the unrealistic pace of progress that, we argue, has led to many of our contemporary eco-social problems. The pace of progress produces an anxiety that we find dangerous. Perhaps the reader is familiar with having too much to do and too little time, and the inevitable, bodily, vision-narrowing stresses that this causes? Perhaps some readers are also existentially concerned about the number of years left in their lives? Perhaps some readers are familiar with the feeling of tension and nervous energy that comes from being late to a meeting or appointment? These are all experiences of the anxiety of chronological time. Such anxiety, we believe, tends to lock us into the efficient narratives of certainty and progress.

The global standardization of time removes people from their location, making each place an empty space that is defined by the abstraction of time devised and determined elsewhere. To notice a sunset while one is walking is to experience a place. To check one's phone to learn the exact time of a sunset and have one's camera ready is to disconnect from that place in multiple ways in the hopes of experiencing it more fully. This is part of the anxiety of time: our daily, embodied locations in place matter less than where we are going and how long it takes us to get there.[2]

Improvisational theater and comedy have something to teach us about living without such anxiety, about reacting to the present with a "yes and" rather than being caught in past memories or anticipations of the future. A documentary about comedian Bill Murray, *The Bill Murray Stories*, suggests that Murray's improvisational background leads him to a semi-Buddhist philosophy emphasizing the central importance of being present, open to whatever happens in the here and now and going with it. The film recounts many stories of Bill Murray sightings in random places in people's daily lives, demonstrating how much he prioritizes surprise and the ability to simply go with the flow of a moment.[3] The present matters far more than what came before and what comes after. In our words, Murray is seeking to embrace the pace of ambiguity, to escape the anxiety of chronological time in order to enjoy the time of the bubbling uncertain present and whatever it brings about.

Many of the world's religious traditions and philosophies have rituals and scriptures that seek to take us out of the illusion of chronological time and pay deep attention to the bubbling up of the present and the cyclical times of the rest of the natural world. Buddhist meditation offers one such example. The annual cycles of liturgy in Catholic and mainline Protestant denominations offer another. Ritual sacrifices and pilgrimages in many Hindu traditions present a similar call to be present, to focus on a particular place, now.

Chronological time produces anxiety because it places all of our thinking into an abstract sense that is literally "out of this world" and "out of this universe." Time, an abstraction, becomes more important than immediate and present relationships. In a world sped up by fossil fuels, the abstraction of time creates a pace of progress that far outstrips the regenerative capacities of the planet, which evolved at their own pace and have no regard for our abstractions.[4] The pace of contemporary, industrialized life has helped to create the problems of climate change, of resource extraction, of extinction. They have taken human lives away from the bubbling present in order to build an imagined, transcendent future. This anxiety of chronological time depends upon efficiency. Our response should involve something different, something less efficient. This is the pace of ambiguity, the ethics of uncertainty, love without reverence.

We make no argument here against chronological time. It makes global coordination possible in amazing ways, and has helped cultures and peoples all over the world to live better lives, to come more fully together, and to cooperate in inspiring ways. But we also deeply value those parts of our lives that pull us out of

112

chronological time, allowing us to experience "flow," to be fully present to another place or another person. And we suggest that perhaps some of our responses to wicked problems should come from the kinds of thinking we do fully in the reality of the present rather than those we do in the abstraction of chronological time.

This is the first vital piece of our answer to the "But what about" questions. All the issues raised by those questions matter deeply. However, because most of us reading this book do not ourselves face those problems *immediately* on most days, our best responses will come if we take deep breaths and notice what is immediate to us, responding from fully realized places rather than abstract spaces. This means leaving room for an ambiguous, meandering, bubbling up sense of time that takes our multiple, globally intersected places seriously rather than subsuming them all into abstract notions of progress or development. Focusing on the uncommon grounds and the uncertain future (salvific or apocalyptic) is going to take becoming comfortable with the uneasiness of an ambiguous pace.

Becoming uneasy

Many of us experience the anxiety of chronological time through our smart devices, calendar alerts, and constant social media updates. With such regular reminders of where we are supposed to be and what we still need to do, it is natural to become uneasy. We develop a sense that we should always be "plugged in" to the mechanisms that enforce chronological time. We feel uneasy when we are separated from the devices that connect us to the abstractions of time and the internet. We also become uneasy with deviating from our schedules or doing things that might "waste" our time. But time can only be "wasted" if it is attached to a notion of progress. If we move away from that narrative, then time spent in the present is never wasted.

To be caught up in progress, in a sense of direction and clarity, creates a sense that every action, every moment should serve some goal. This leads to an ever-quickening pace, a desire to always accomplish more, to be more efficient. At its worst, this habit of mind reduces even our relationships to means rather than ends, treating other people as a "standing reserve" of resources that will help us reach our goals.[5] Perhaps, in a world as complex as that in which industrialized people live in the 21st century, we all need to do this sometimes in order to get through our days. But what happens when this is the only sense of time we experience and think about? Might our desire to "get things done" have contributed to many of the wicked problems of our age? If so, how might we learn to stop being so uneasy about living fully in the ambiguous present?

Perhaps if we want to stay with the present embodiment in time-space, we might learn to also become uneasy with the pace of progress. Perhaps such uneasiness will help us to be more comfortable with the particular moments in which we live, open to our relationships and present realities, accepting of ambiguity.

In the book *In A Queer Time and Place*, Jack Halberstam argues that the reproduction of chronological time participates in the heteronormative reproduction of families, generation after generation.[6] In other words, the reproduction of the (nuclear) family and its ideals of "tradition" has helped to keep people locked into a certain sense of time and progress. This has led to the exclusion and oppression of those "queer" persons who do not live into the heteronormative model of life. Learning from people like Halberstam, this book has sought not to oppress queer perspectives, but to learn from them. What approach to time—and to space and to ethics and to love—might we find if we take our instructions from those who seem queer, whose uneasiness with traditions makes traditions uneasy? In other words, if the time scale of a life is not focused on the reproduction of a certain type of family, or reproducing the status quo of a heteronormative society, then what might a life's time look like? As we have learned to accept multiple approaches to love and to family, perhaps we need to embrace multiple times, to live with queer, uncommon understandings of chronology.

To the extent that we want an organized world that maintains familiar traditions and supports the "way things have always been," such queer ideas of time will make us uneasy. But the organized, traditional world is unsustainable and oppressive. We need to learn to become uneasy with it, to embrace that uneasiness, and to move on.

Learning from the undercommons

Time as most of us in the industrialized world know it and live by it was globally standardized in the middle of the 20th century.[7] Before this, time was a much more local, particular to places. It remains this way for those who live outside of industrial structures, whose lives are—by choice or necessity—shaped more by the rising and setting of the sun and atmospheric change than by watches and calendars. These lives follow the light, seasons, stars and moon to understand what should be done and when. Time is understood by the immediate activities and interactions that make up life. Time is related intimately to place (just ask any farmer), which for those of us with globalized lives is an uncommon experience.

We do not seek to romanticize pre-industrial life. But we do seek to notice a sense of time that has been largely lost by those of us who live in industrial, standardized time. To institute common time, people had to embrace the transcendent, accepting standardized abstractions over daily experience. Embodied markers were evacuated of relevancy and agency.

In other words, chronological time creates a commons that, like most commons, elides and conceals the undercommons.[8] This idea, which we explored in Chapter 1, is spelled out by Stefano Harney and Fred Moten in *The Undercommons: Fugitive Planning and Black Study*. Drawing on the voices and the wisdom of the neglected and abjected undercommons, Harney and Moten critique the efficiency of chronological time and ideals of progress by focusing on "planning" in industrialized structures. They note that "planning," both in the capitalist world many of us live in and the state socialist structures that used to be imagined as the alternative, is opposed to real human action:

> Planning in the undercommons is not an activity, not fishing or dancing or teaching or loving, but the ceaseless experiment with the futurial presence of the forms of life that make such activities possible. It is these means that were eventually stolen by, in having been willingly given up to, state socialism whose perversion of planning was a crime second only to the deployment of policy in today's command economy.[9]

To "plan" in this sense is to create a community by excluding others, to create a commons that inevitably leaves out an undercommons. Harney and Moten advocate an antagonism toward any such commons. Lifting up the undercommons means continually tripping up the hoped for "common" outcome or "common" grounds, which are always built on the rubble of some undercommons.

As Catherine Keller notes, "The undercommons names a public that has lost hope in politics but that persists in resistance and self-organization. It can hardly be deemed apolitical, even if it refuses any nominal politics."[10] We understand the politics of the undercommons to include resistance against the tyranny of chronological time, particularly when this sense of time is caught up in and shaped by fossil-fueled "progress." The reality of the undercommons calls on all who can to see many different times and many different places as combined but not subsumed into a diverse and multitudinous planetary community.

A resonant concept is the theory of "Rainbow Gravity," which posits a kind of particle-based perspectivism based on the fact that color influences energetic behavior. As Clara Moskowitz explains it, "The color of light is determined by its frequency, and because different frequencies correspond to different energies, light particles (photons) of different colors would travel on slightly different paths through spacetime, according to their energy."[11] Different frequencies and different paths through space-time mean different embodiments and multiple ways of becoming. This resonates with the "prismatic ecology" discussed in our first chapter, suggesting that there must also be multiple ways of being an environmentalist.

To connect environmentalism to the frequencies of light is highly speculative, but speculation is precisely what makes new ways of becoming possible. As geographer Kathryn Yussoff points out, the world we live in has been fundamentally shaped by people who assumed "Whiteness as the color of universality."[12] To push against this, to create a different future, will require the ability to see many different colors and to recognize that none is universal. We need spectral thinking to discern a spectrum of possibilities.

Gravity helps to position bodies in different ways of becoming, and thus helps to diffract on the pluralistic ethics and politics that become possible in different planetary contexts. In other words, just as there is never one commons; just as no one set of beliefs, meanings, and values can apply to all in the same way; so there cannot be a single, common way of moving forward in space-time from the planetary present. This means that our ethics at the pace of ambiguity must adopt an un-apocalyptic and unsalvific understanding of the future.

Thinking un-apocalyptically

As discussed earlier in the book, environmental historian Carolyn Merchant provides a good critique of the narratives of Recovery, Progress and Decline that are often found not only in western Christian narratives of time and reality, but also in the background of those working for social and/or ecological justice. In all cases, the idea is that things are slowly progressing from chaos to order or declining from paradise to degradation.[13] This overlay of the arrow of chronological time creates several problems in terms of thinking about the planet at the pace of ambiguity.

The very existence of multiple narratives of Progress and Decline reveals that reality is more complicated than any imagined Paradise or Apocalypse. There is no single trajectory, no simplistic direction of history. Any declensionist or progressive narrative is an interpretation that ignores or leaves out much of life. Cosmic history includes the creation and death of stars, the expansion and retraction of space; there is no one narrative. Natural history includes diverging evolutionary paths of slow and drastic change; there is no one narrative. Climatic history includes times of stability and times of drastic change; there is no one narrative. There are always multiple stories to be told about time.

If we seek to find just one overarching story we will always be tempted to put ourselves in the center of it, to suggest that the universe and the earth and the climate are here for *homo sapiens*, or at least some homo sapiens. Those who believe in the steady progress of the universe toward the present too often suggest that human beings are the pinnacle of creation. Those who believe in a steady decline of civilization in our time too often suggest that the greatest tragedy in the universe would be for life to become more difficult for industrialized humans. In both cases, our species or some subset of it is used as the measure. Of course it is always important to measure things based on our own experience, but it is equally important to remind ourselves of the limitations of doing so.

Any narrative of progress or decline sets a direction for certain people or other planetary entities. This, again, overlooks the undercommons that are composted in order to claim progressive ground. One is reminded here also of the early evolutionary trees and charts in the late 19th and early 20th centuries that placed European culture and language at the top of evolutionary development. We believe apocalyptic and salvific narratives are dangerous unless they are multiplied, unless we simultaneously embrace many of them.

It is important to notice an apocalypse. For example, it is vital to mourn and repent for the many ways that the lives and realities of indigenous communities across the world have been ended by the colonialist expansion of European peoples.[14] It is also important to note progress. For example, it is worthwhile to celebrate the accomplishments of human reason in changing the world around

116

us and in vastly improving some lives.[15] Both narratives contain truth. Even if some truths are more urgent than others, none is the complete truth on its own. We must bring the apocalyptic into conversation with the un-apoc-alyptic; the progressive into conversation with the unprogressive.

Any single narrative also runs the risk of inspiring fatalism. In other words, reading the world in terms of a certain chronological time-scale that is progressive or in decline creates a self-fulfilling prophecy: progress and decline begin to feel all but inevitable, so our actions come to matter less. If progress is inevitable, we can relax, things will get better, it is taken care of. If decline is inevitable, we can relax, things cannot be saved, we should eat, drink, and be merry.

The universality of imperfection

Un-apocalpytic attention to the undercommons leaves us, the authors of this book, uneasy with the traditional pace of progress. And yet we are stuck within that pace, because we want to meet the deadline for publication of this book but also need time to grade papers we have been putting off and want to finish both in time to meet our partners for a pleasant meal. Even as we are suspicious of chronological time, we are caught within it, and we have no intention of extracting ourselves. The final step in our concluding embrace of ambiguity, then, needs to be an acceptance of universal imperfection.

All environmental ethics is imperfect, and all environmentalists are imperfect. This is captured well by a phrase that has been part of the North American environmental movement since its foundations: "We have met the enemy and he [sic] is us." Cartoonist Walt Kelly wrote this on a poster for the first Earth Day celebration in 1970, attributing the phrase to his character Pogo, an anthropomorphic possum. The slogan reflects the fact that environmental challenges indict anyone in an industrialized culture who has enough privilege and wealth to learn about them. The energy and resources it takes to under-stand and to protest environmental degradation contribute to that degradation, as does the daily life of most of us reading these words who use fossil fuels, eating food and wearing clothes that we have not made ourselves. To study environmental ethics is to understand oneself as part of the problem.

Not all environmentalists embrace this truth. Some seek to purify themselves, to separate themselves from the causes of degradation. Some model their lives on the ascetics of past eras, who have foregone comforts and privileges in order to separate themselves from society and its imperfections. They stop using fossil fuels in any form, banish plastic from their lives, grow their own food, or head for a life in undeveloped territory or with non-industrial peoples.[16] We have much to learn from such brave witnesses, among other things the ways we can all reduce our footprint on the earth and our complicity in serious problems when we do not.

But we must also be wary of narratives that suggest anyone in the indus-trialized world can and should truly remove themselves from complicity in environmental challenges. Alexis Shotwell argues in *Against Purity* that the trend toward "purism" in the environmental movement and others like it is dangerous because it creates a "de-collectivizing, de-mobilizing, paradoxical politics of despair."[17] Shotwell raises two concerns here. First, attempting to purify oneself is "de-collectivizing" because it separates the self from the community, seeking purity for "me" rather than improvement for "us." Shotwell notices a symptom of this in "*self*-righteous politics startlingly in line with conspiracy theories; what matters is whether you, individually, have the correct language, analysis, critique."[18] At their worst, purists seek to present themselves as having the most evolved, complex or "progressive" ideas, from which others should learn. These are individualistic ideals, and also assume an ideal of "progress" that asserts linearity and monolithic ideas of what is good and right. This is not helpful. All humans, all beings, are in this together. We will not solve our collective problems individually, and we can only understand the complexity of our world when we do so in community.

Second, purism is "de-mobilizing" because it is doomed to failure. Anyone in the industrialized world conditioned and shaped by racism and patriarchy who tries to enitrely free themselves from these mistakes will fail as long as they maintain any connection to the society itself. As people struggle for purity and fail, they find how deep their complicity goes, creating frustration and discouraging any action at all. Healthy engagement, Shotwell argues, requires that people "perceive complexity and complicity as the constitutive situation of our lives."[19] We are part of the problem; we are "the enemy." Accepting that—and the unease it creates—is the beginning of deciding what to do.

While we believe we have much to learn from those who seek to live purer and better lives, and while we seek to eat and shop and travel as responsibly as we can, the authors of this book have not chosen ascetic lifestyles. We devote our energies to changing the society we live in rather than removing ourselves from it. In so doing, we embrace our own imperfections. We accept that we are "the enemy" when it comes to environmental degradation—just as we could be seen as "the enemy" as participants in patriarchy, white supremacy, capitalism, and many other wicked problems. It is not fun to be the enemy, and it gives us no pride. But it underlines the ambiguity of our reality and thus, we hope, leads us to better action.

Imperfection is universal. This gives no one permission to do harm or to fail to do our best to do good. People should strive to be better. But people should also strive to accept that we will never be perfect, never be pure. Perfection and purity are further expressions of the certainty that this book has argued against. Perfection and purity are goals toward which some people delude themselves they can "progress," with all the limitations and failings that come along with such a focused vision. Here and now, in our present reality, no human being is perfect. Accepting that, and thereby accepting our own imperfections, is an important step to living in the present, with our own imperfections and those around us. Living with our own imperfections and the imperfect societies and institutions that shape us means separating ourselves from the sweeping progressive and declensionist narratives of chronological time. It helps us understand that there is no simplistic "forward" or "backward;" the world is far more complicated and uncertain.

Environmental ethics in uncommon times

If environmentalism is a community of ongoing conversations, then no voice should be allowed to dominate, no perspective should be unquestioned. A conversation about climate change is far more than any single argument. A conversation about ambiguity is a starting point for action and a starting point for slowing down and stopping the wrong kinds of action.

Many religious traditions celebrate practices of inaction: slowing down, meditating, doing and consuming less, and deep contemplation are all as much about *avoiding* behaviors as embracing them. Such inaction may at times be more generative and creative than immediately jumping to action. If we are to transition beyond the fast-paced chronological progress of a fossil-fueled reality, we will need to learn some of these practices of slowing down and paying deep attention to the world around us. This is not a turn toward a progressive and certain future, but toward our planetary community made up of a wild diversity of human and earth others.

This theoretical conclusion has argued that part of this "slowing down" must include a critical uneasiness with straightforwardly chronological understandings of time. In a diverse conversation about complex environmental problems, we must recognize the different time scales at which life moves. One size does not fit all, just as one solution will not fit all.

We suggest that a fossil-fueled reality is simply too fast. It discourages careful attention, it prevents deliberate organization of a life that includes genuine openness to the planetary community. This is a broad critique of industrial civilization, its paces, and its injustices. As the previous chapters have shown, the pace of progress is unfair and oppressive. Those of us who live sped up lives do so at the expense of other places, which are often forced to live "slower" and to believe that this is a deficit. Those of us fueled by carbon move quickly past the damage we cause in the world, damage to those who live without that speed who often suffer from our pollution and overconsumption.[20]

Our critique of fossil-fueled pacing also raises deeply personal questions about how our own individual lives contribute to environmental problems on a daily basis. Wherever we are on the planet, we are located in global flows of energy, matter, and information. These shape our lives, but we also shape them. And when we insist on a slower pace, even in one small aspect of our lives, it makes a difference. Efforts to reduce one's carbon footprint, or to take on a practice of meditation, or to eat lower on the food chain, are all small ways to resist the speed of fossil-fueled reality. Making such moves helps others to share their uneasiness with the anxiety of chronological time. It reveals and empowers the hidden undercommons, at least a little bit. It uncovers the un-apocalyptic aspects of life that endure, and encourages us to embrace the universality of imperfection. Our actions matter, and so our final chapter turns to difficult, and uncertain, questions of individual and collective action.

Notes

1 Hulme, *Why We Disagree About Climate Change*, 359.
2 This increase in the pace of time that outstrips the carrying capacity of the planet, and even the capacity of embodied human beings is what some have called the great acceleration. See McNeill & Engelke, *The Great Acceleration*.
3 Avallone, *The Bill Murray Stories*.
4 Brennan, *Globalization and Its Terrors*.
5 Heidegger, *Question Concerning Technology and Other Essays*, 3–35.
6 Halberstam, *In a Queer Time and Place*.
7 Ogle, *The Global Transformation of Time 1870–1950*.
8 Harney & Moten, *The Undercommons*.
9 Ibid., 74–75.
10 Keller, *Political Theology of the Earth*, 31.
11 See Clara Moskowitz, "In a 'Rainbow' Universe, Time May Have No Beginning," *Scientific American*, December 9, 2013, http://www.scientificamerican.com/article/rainbow-gravity-universe-beginning/.
12 Yusoff, *A Billion Black Anthropocenes or None*, 51.
13 Merchant, *Reinventing Eden*.
14 Whyte, "Is it Colonial Déja Vu?"
15 Abrams, *A God That Could be Real*.
16 See, for example, O'Brien, *Violence of Climate Change*, Ch. 3.
17 Shotwell, *Against Purity*, 9.
18 Ibid., 196. Emphasis in original.
19 Ibid., 8
20 Val Plumwood argues that part of the problem with contemporary politics is that those closest to environmental and social problems are the ones with least power and those in power are the ones least affected by it. See Plumwood, *Environmental Culture*, 34.

CONCLUDING PRACTICES FOR AN UNCERTAIN STAND

Fracking, protesting, and engineering the climate

with Richard Bohannon

Anyone who believes they have *the* answer to the major environmental problems of the 21st century is part of the problem. We have tried to make this argument throughout this book, suggesting that seeking globalized progress contributes to the dangerous pace and direction of contemporary life. We have argued that anyone who looks for moral absolutes contributes to the dangerous quest for certainty that marginalizes others. We have explored the dangers of unambiguous emotional responses to environmental problems, arguing that complexity always requires multiple perspectives and an irreverent awareness of our own limits.

While the other even-numbered chapters have sought practical guidance in how to live out such an ethics of uncertainty from historical figures, this concluding one will instead seek practical wisdom in the face of contemporary climate-related questions: how to respond to the increase in fracking methods to extract oil and natural gas, to the growing movement of climate protests, and to the prospects of climate engineering. The political and scientific realities about these issues will certainly change between our writing and your reading, but we hope that working out our argument on these issues as we understand them will demonstrate what it looks like to take a stand while holding an ethics of uncertainty.

The uncertainties of fracking

Hydraulic fracturing, commonly called "fracking," is an increasingly common set of drilling methods that allows access to oil and natural gas that were previously believed out of reach or economically unprofitable. Miners first drill vertically to the depth of the deposit—often more than a mile below the surface—and then drill horizontally through rock deposits saturated with petroleum and/or natural gas. A solution of water, lubricating chemicals and sand is then pumped through the well and into the deposit, causing fissures through which the oil or gas can flow and be extracted.

The concept of hydraulic fracturing dates back as far as the 1860s, when nitroglycerin was first used to stimulate the flow of oil wells, and was first used commercially in 1949, by Halliburton.[1] By the 1980s, fracking was a common means used to extend the life of existing conventional wells. In the 1990s, the combination of horizontal drilling with hydraulic fracturing was first used to extract natural gas from previously untapped supplies in Texas's Barnett Shale formation, and the practice has since expanded dramatically. At the time of this writing, fracking is primarily used in the United States, but also on a more limited scale in Australia, several European countries, Russia and China.

As Rebecca Lave and Brian Lutz have noted, fracking is "perhaps the most substantive change in the landscape and practice of energy production in the U.S. since the advent of the fossil fuel economy."[2] While none of the individual components of technology are new, the combination and the refinement of existing technologies have opened up vast oil and gas deposits that could not previously have been extracted at a profit. For example, in the Bakken region of North Dakota and Montana, geologists have known about oil deposits since the early 20th century, and a relatively small amount of oil has been extracted there for decades. However, most of that oil was considered inaccessible because traditional drilling techniques would have been prohibitively expensive. Most of it is two miles beneath the surface, and conventional drilling would have required "hundreds or thousands more wellbores" to reach the disparate deposits. Pre-fracking oil production in North Dakota peaked in the mid-1980s at about 4.5 million barrels of oil produced, per month, and had declined to between 2.5 and 3.0 million barrels per month by the early 2000s. The state's oil production for December 2018, in contrast, was a record 43.44 million barrels,[3] the increase almost entirely the result of modern fracking technology.

Why fracking is a bad idea

To grapple with fracking is to grapple with environmental uncertainty. Because these methods are relatively new, we do not fully understand their ecological impacts.[4] Most research to date has focused on issues of water quality, because the flushing procedures involved in fracking use enormous quantities of water with added chemicals.[5] But even extensive research leaves more questions than answers. The exact composition of the chemicals used are considered proprietary to oil and gas companies, and so most of the public does not know exactly what has been pumped under the ground. Reports differ on how much danger these chemicals pose to groundwater supplies. Fracking advocates insist that they drill so far beneath water tables at such high pressure that no chemicals will ever come into water supplies, but critics note that the flushing process brings water back up to the surface along with not only traces of fracking chemicals, but also salts and toxic and radioactive materials from deep underground. Spills and storage errors can certainly lead to water contaminated by the chemicals used in fracking, but advocates insist that careful industrial practice reduces that risk to virtual negligibility.[6]

T. Boone Pickens, a prominent energy magnate and billionaire, unflaggingly insists that fracking is safe. He notes that he has "fracked over a thousand wells" and "never had a failure on one of them." In 2015, he reported that his own ranch in Texas had 44 fracking wells drilled on it, and he was planning for 62 more.[7] Pickens insists that natural gas is the "fuel of the future" and a vital path toward freedom from imported oil in the United States, and so he enthusiastically advocates fracking for natural gas as part of a national energy strategy.[8]

Insofar as Pickens's confidence in fracking is absolute, insofar as he is *certain* that fracking should be a part of the future and that past fracking in existing wells guarantees the safety of future practices, he is engaging in exactly the kind of thinking we have critiqued throughout this book. Confident that the world is more complicated than Pickens admits and that the economics of energy production are less predictable than he sees, we are skeptical of his proposal.

Even separate from the issues of water contamination, fracking comes with environmental costs. Drilling disrupts ecosystems, —for instance, natural gas extraction in Pennsylvania's Marcellus shale has led to widespread forest fragmentation, and the noise, light, and air pollution of any huge industrial activity will always affect ecological processes[9]—threatens vulnerable species, and causes earthquakes in some areas, including Oklahoma and Alberta.[10]

Perhaps the most important argument against fracking is that it offers access to supplies of oil and natural gas that were previously going to be left in the ground. If those fossil fuels are extracted and burned, they will contribute even further to a changing climate, worsening the impact of humanity upon our atmosphere and increasing the chances of a bleaker future. While it is common to hear arguments that natural gas should replace coal because it emits less CO_2 into the atmosphere when burned, this ignores the fact that natural gas wellpads often leak substantial amounts of methane, another highly reactive climate changing gas.[11]

Environmentally speaking, fracking is a bad idea, and no environmental ethics should deny this fact. The authors of this chapter are against fracking, and we would happily vote for a nationwide or international ban. Short of that, we would resolutely protest against hydraulic fracking permits being issued by any community in which we have the authority to speak out. Our ethics of ambiguity does not prevent us from taking these stands.

Why not fracking might be a bad idea, too

However, the particular ethical approach of this book insists that we also admit that *not* fracking could be a bad idea, too. An ethics of ambiguity allows no simple moral calculus; it rejects any simple answers to the moral challenges of environmental degradation.

Allison Chin, the president of the Sierra Club, offered a clear argument against fracking in 2012: "If drillers can't extract natural gas without destroying landscapes and endangering the health of families, then we should not drill for natural gas."[12] We agree with the sentiment, but are more cautious about the specifics, because we are not sure that there is such thing as a completely non-destructive form of energy production in a technological civilization. Even solar and wind technologies have health and environmental costs, relying on the mining of copper and rare minerals and causing habitat loss and fragmentation. While we admit that fracking for natural gas currently runs the risk of destroying landscapes and endangering human health, we find it too simplistic to suggest that *any* method with such impacts should be disqualified; that is too certain a statement and there are no impact-free options. Furthermore, we are not certain that we have the authority to decide that *no one* should be fracking for natural gas; we simply do not know enough to make such a categorical statement.

It is clear that fracking disrupts habitats, stresses ecosystems, raises earthquake risks, endangers water supplies, and contributes to further climate change. Fracking is a bad idea. But those of us who oppose fracking must face the question of what will be done instead. In the current energy economy of the United States, the most likely answer is that if we stop fracking we will burn more coal. Since the onset of natural gas fracking, the demand for coal has gone down, and some coal plants have been converted to instead burn natural gas. This is a move from one fossil fuel to another, but it is beneficial. While leaked methane likely nullifies the ecological advantage that natural gas burns far more cleanly than coal, fracking still seems less environmentally destructive than the strip mining and mountaintop removal commonly used to extract coal. Proponents of fracking therefore argue that the best and most realistic way to reduce greenhouse gas emissions, at least temporarily, is to extract more natural gas rather than less, using whatever methods are most efficient. Furthermore, fracking for oil may be less damaging to habitats than conventional oil production, because it requires fewer drilled holes at the surface level.

Fracking has made oil and natural gas cheaper. This has led to less coal extraction, which is a positive development. Less expensive oil and natural gas is, of course, also bad for the climate insofar as it encourages more driving, more energy usage, and more consumption. But despite these facts, lower prices are good in the short term for people who struggle to make financial ends meet. Critics of fossil fuels believe that they are ultimately destructive and have led to grossly uneven distribution of wealth. But abundant and affordable fossil fuels can still help poor and working-class people. Any argument about fracking that does not admit this is incomplete. It does not mean that fracking is good, or even a good idea; but it does mean that the moral question of fracking is not simplistic.

The environmental community does not need to wrestle with the question of whether fracking is bad. It is. A more important question is also more ambiguous: "Is not fracking better than fracking?" We hesitantly answer in the affirmative once again, but only after wrestling with not only the clear environmental harms of fracking, but also the potential environmental costs of not fracking if that leads to more coal extraction. We need to wrestle with the immediate impacts on poor peoples and poor nations if fossil fuels become more expensive as they become harder to extract. And we need to wrestle with the fact that no one can be sure how quickly or how fully renewable energies could be made to replace fossil fuel sources. We oppose fracking, but ambiguously.

Climate protests

Resistance to fracking is one example of a broader movement across the world that is speaking out resolutely against the extraction and the use of fossil fuels. Another strand of that movement works against oil pipelines, pointing out the dangers of transporting fossil fuels across vast expanses and working to deny permits in order to make production and distribution more expensive and therefore more rare. In 2014, the Dakota Access Corporation announced a project to build an oil pipeline from North Dakota to a refinery in Illinois. The goal was a pipeline that would move around 500,000 barrels of oil per day from the Bakken oil fields, much of which was otherwise transported by rail cars. Protesters soon began pointing out that this pipeline would pose dangers to local water supplies. The most prominent among these voices were those of the Standing Rock Sioux, whose reservation was near the pipeline's route and who said their health—already endangered by centuries of colonial oppression—would be threatened by potential oil spills. Labeling themselves "Water Protectors," the Standing Rock Sioux set up a protest camp near the Missouri River, attracting international attention and widespread solidarity from other indigenous groups and environmental organizations. In December of that year, many of those protestors felt vindicated when the Army Corps of Engineers denied an easement for part of the permit, forcing the corporation to begin considering changes in the pipeline's route. However, in 2017 President Trump approved the final construction, and by the end of that year, oil was flowing and leaks had already been reported.[13]

Still another strand of climate protests involves children standing up against what they see as criminal negligence by adults who have failed to respond to the climate emergency. In August of 2018, the Swedish ninth-grader Greta Thunberg stopped attending school in order to protest outside the Swedish parliament, holding a sign that said *Skolstrejk för klimatet* ("School strike for the climate.") By the end of that year, thousands of students all over Europe and the United States were refusing to attend school on Fridays, and as of this writing similar strikes are taking shape all over the world. In a TEDx talk, Thunberg explained that she no longer trusted adults who talked about long-term policies or plans for the climate and asked children to have hope for the future: "Yes, we do need hope—of course, we do. But the one thing we need more than hope is action. Once we start to act, hope is everywhere." Such action might require dramatic change, as she asserted in a forceful speech to a 2018 climate conference in Poland: "If solutions within the system are so impossible to find, then maybe we should change the system itself."[14] For Thunberg and for thousands of other students around the world, hope comes from protest actions that demand radical change, and each week they emphasize that climate action is more important to their future than the education provided in their schools.

Why not protesting would be a bad idea

The inspirational figures of social activism cited in earlier chapters left a legacy continued by these protestors. The Standing Rock Sioux standing up for water and human life continue the legacy of Marjory Stoneman Douglas and their protest against a system of racialized oppression extends the human rights work of Malcolm X. Thunberg and other students are nonviolently calling for change in a way resonant with Martin Luther King, Jr.'s tactics, and their use of science to make social and political arguments builds on the work of Rachel Carson.

It would be anachronistic to assert that any of the historical figures just mentioned would have been part of these protests—what they would think and what they would do if they were alive today is unknowable, and the records of what they actually did and said are impressive enough without having to speculate. However, our reading of those figures does influence us to feel supportive of and empowered by contemporary protests. Seeking to continue the kinds of social action that Malcolm X, Martin Luther King, Rachel Carson, and Marjory Stoneman Douglas modeled, we applaud and draw inspiration from the 21st century environmentalists who stood with Standing Rock and the students who demand that their leaders act.

The Standing Rock Sioux identified their protest camp as "a first of its kind gathering of Indigenous Nations. The most recent such assembly occurred when the Great Sioux Nation gathered before the Battle at the Little Big Horn."[15] Anyone who believed that environmental issues were solely the interest of privileged white people saw that this was not true if they paid attention to Standing Rock. Anyone who had never wrestled with the connections between colonialism and fossil fuel extraction was shown the connections if they paid attention to Standing Rock. Anyone who had not stood up for the rights of indigenous peoples to control their lives and their land was asked to do so.

Many thousands answered that call, and the diverse group that gathered to support the Sioux emphasized that they were motivated not only by the pipeline, but also the legacy of oppression. Among these supporters were a group of predominantly white military veterans who pledged to support and, if needed, defend the Water Protectors. While police used brutal tactics to try to control the protestors, the gathering of native peoples, environmental activists, and veterans united for a peaceful protest, and took time for a ceremony in which veterans offered a formal apology for the ways the military had treated natives in its past. Joseph Pritchard, an Air Force veteran who served in the Viet Nam War reported that he was "blown away" by the "movement of prayer" at

126

Standing Rock, and had learned "that if we just stand up and we just show up and work together we can change things for the better."[16]

In similar ways, the global climate movement is being inspired by student protesters as we write these words. Longtime climate journalist and activist Bill McKibben called Thunberg's strike "a terrific idea," and praised the "leadership from the youngest people in this fight."[17] In the Netherlands, 350 scientists signed an open letter supporting Dutch student strikers. These scientists not only aligned themselves to the students, they were also inspired to use their authority as experts to advocate for political change: "On the basis of the facts supplied by climate science, the campaigners are right" and "We cannot permit ourselves any longer to wait before taking the necessary measures."[18]

Like the standing rock protests, the activism of students makes connections between climate change and justice. The movement has been led almost entirely by young women and girls, demonstrating not only that future generations want action, but also that such action will need to come from thinking outside of patriarchal and gender-normative power structures. Anuna De Wever, a 17-year old from Belgium, was inspired by Greta Thunberg to lead a protest that included up to 30,000 people. Assigned female gender at birth, De Wever identified as a boy throughout primary school and then in her teens began to identify as gender-fluid and to prefer female pronouns. She notes that her experience with gender helped to fuel this work: "I don't look at the mainstream and what they think. I start to have my own values, own principles, and I think about what's not going right in this world and what I can do to improve it instead of just closing my eyes to it."[19] Protestors in Belgium, Sweden, and around the world are following young women and non-binary leaders, demonstrating that a different future is possible.

The energy, momentum, and empowerment that comes from these protests is good, and leads us to not only applaud these protestors' accomplishments but also to advocate further protests against fossil fuel extraction and climate inaction.

Why protesting might be a bad idea

Our commitment to uncertainty remains, though, and while it does not change our support for protests, it does mean that such support is not our last word. Protests are good, but they are not unambiguously so; there are real risks in the prominent place such actions are taking in the environmental movement.

In 2015, then-President Barack Obama denied a permit to extend the Keystone Pipeline after years of protest, including an enormous nonviolent action at the White House that led to over 1,000 arrests and substantial media attention. In his speech rejecting the Keystone Pipeline extension, President Obama made no mention of the protestors who had been seeking his attention for over five years. Instead, he emphasized that rejecting the pipeline came from his confidence that investment and development of new technologies could make a clean energy future possible. He asserted that "this is America, and we have to come up with new ways and new technologies to break down the old rules, so that today, homegrown American energy is booming, energy prices are falling, and over the past decade, even as our economy has continued to grow, America has cut our total carbon pollution more than any other country on earth." As framed in this statement, the President was motivated not by activist protests but by economic and technological information. One can even detect a critique of protestors in the statement, as when he said that Keystone had come to occupy "an overinflated role in our political discourse... . This obscured the fact that this pipeline would neither be a silver bullet for the economy, as was promised by some, nor the express lane to climate disaster proclaimed by others."[20]

Of course the fact that President Obama did not directly mention protestors does not mean they had no influence upon his decision, but it is worth seriously considering the rhetoric of a seasoned organizer who became President and then declined to credit other organizers for his decision. It is also worth noting that, upon entering office a year after Obama denied this permit, President Trump began finding ways to authorize it. So, it is at least possible that the environmental movement might have focused too much on pipelines, and could instead consider more economic analysis and technological innovation.

The other question requiring some analysis is whether the demand for alternatives is sufficient to make such alternatives a reality. Pipeline protestors generally hope to keep fossil fuels "in the ground," but the oil industry repeatedly asserts that they will not leave oil where it is, even if they are denied pipelines. They will, instead, put it on trains, which are far more likely to explode or leak than a devoted pipeline. The CEO of TransCanada released a statement with this veiled threat in August of 2016, saying "We think Canadians would rather have a pipeline buried four feet underground than trains loaded with oil driving through the heart of homes and neighbourhoods."[21] We do not trust oil executives to tell the whole truth about their business interests. But we do trust them to work tirelessly to pump and sell oil, and to be willing to put that oil on a train if they cannot put it in a pipeline. The dangers of oil trains are not imagined: in July, 2013, a train carrying oil from the Bakken region exploded in the center of Lac-Mégantic, Quebec, killing 47 people and destroying its downtown. Not only does avoiding pipelines increase dangers, it also increases costs: if oil companies must simply pay more to transport their product, they will pass these costs on to customers, and the poorest will be hit hardest.

Greta Thunberg responds to this troubling reality by calling to change "the system itself." If oil companies can find ways around pipeline bans, then a deeper look must be taken at whether corporate structures and current property regimes are sustainable and just. They are not, as revealed by the racist colonial governance that made Standing Rock protests necessary. Deeper changes are essential; but deeper changes are, inherently, more difficult.

Our argument has been that such deep changes will never fit into a slogan. Protesting is a good idea, but like all other goods, it is only ambiguously and partially good. It must be complemented by deep study, detailed organization and conversation, and patience for the slow process of ambiguous improvement.

It is brave to travel to Washington DC for an arrest action, to join the Water Protectors in North Dakota, to leave school to protest against political inaction. But in a finite and complicated world, these actions take time away from other possibilities. Anyone who claims that a protest is an unambiguous good, is the only right action, is working from a model of certainty.

Climate engineering

While protestors focus on political and social change, others assume that the best hope for humanity's future in a world of climate change is technological, and that this will require the speedy deployment of large-scale technologies that carefully repair some of the damage that industrial activity has done so carelessly for centuries.[22]

There are two broad approaches to climate engineering. The first is "Solar Radiation Management," which seeks to reflect some of the sun's light and heat back into space and thereby offset warming. The most popular proposals tend to involve adding artificial clouds to the earth's stratosphere, which would be more reflective than other surfaces and thereby reduce global temperatures. While this would not do anything about the underlying causes of climate change—the atmosphere would still be filled with heat-trapping gases—it would offset the impacts somewhat by reducing average global temperatures.

Other proposals focus on preventing the most prevalent climate changing gas, CO_2, from being emitted and changing the atmosphere in the first place. The most popular of these proposals is called "Bioenergy with Carbon Capture and Storage," which proposes to move energy production away from fossil fuels and toward plants like palm, switchgrass, or corn. These renewable crops can be burned to meet energy needs, and then new technologies would capture their emissions and bury them deep underground rather than allowing them to be put into the air.

In both cases, people propose to develop new, enormous and ambitious technologies to regulate or limit the changing climate. Very few people advocate climate engineering as the only solution to climate change, but it is increasingly common to see experts arguing that such technologies will be necessary at least to allow some time before political and social change can solidify truly renewable energy sources and change human consumption patterns. For example, in the Intergovernmental Panel on Climate Change's 2018 report on how the global community could limit average warming to 1.5 °C, the panel presents four "pathways" to the future, each of which requires the removal of between 100–1000 billion tons of CO_2 from the atmosphere in the 21st century. Three of the four assume that Bioenergy with Carbon Capture and Storage technologies will be quickly developed and scaled up to make this possible.[23]

Why engineering the climate is a bad idea

We believe that engineering the climate is a bad idea. In almost every proposal of which we are aware, climate engineering would continue the managerial, progress-obsessed, and colonial mistakes that led to climate change in the first place, while providing an excuse for those who seek to continue destructive, polluting practices unchecked.

If climate change is the tragic, logical outcome of Western ideals of dominance and hierarchy, then climate engineering would simply continue the fundamental mistakes that led to the problem. For centuries, Westerners have believed that the world should meet our needs, and this has led us to see everything around us as a "resource" to be managed rather than a subject worthy of respect, an attitude that we have too-often extended even to our fellow human beings. We have been overconfident that these "resources" did not matter on their own, and that we could simplistically manage them. We have been wrong. Climate engineering seems largely like a continuation of such thinking, treating the atmosphere as a resource and a tool with which to solve human problems rather than a system to be respected on its own terms. It is more of a way to continue industrial management than to undo it. This is clearly suggested by the fact that political voices that have long been opposed to any political or economic response to climate change appear open to considering climate engineering.[24]

Climate engineering proposals also tend to depend upon narratives of human technological progress which we have repeatedly criticized in this book. For example, the Harvard scientist David Keith is a prominent advocate of climate engineering research. He runs a research team at Harvard that is experimenting with solar radiation management and founded a private company that is developing carbon capture technologies.[25] Keith admits that climate engineering is not ideal, but he also seems excited about the ways it will show off human brilliance and ingenuity. In the conclusion to his book, *A Case for Climate Engineering*, he writes:

> About a million years after inventing stone cutting tools, ten thousand years after agriculture, and a century after the Wright Brothers flight, humanity's instinct for collaborative tool building has brought us the ability to manipulate our own genome and our planet's climate... We may use these powers for good or ill, but it is hard not to delight in these newfound tools as an expression of collaborative human effort to understand the natural world.[26]

It is worth resisting the urge to delight in these tools when they are presented as the natural outcome of human progress. Progress is a dangerous narrative of certainty, creating problems rather than solving them.

It is also worth asking whether climate engineering could really be as "collaborative" as Keith suggests, whether the political systems that have so far failed to create any globally unified response to climate change could ever regulate and monitor technologies that intentionally reshape the global atmosphere and temperature. Technological concerns aside, could social systems be built that would empower people to genuinely and justly understand, participate in, and give their consent to climate engineering technologies? Potawatomi scholar and activist Kyle Powys Whyte suggests not, arguing that indigenous peoples have important experience with others making decisions about the territories they inhabit and over which they are legally sovereign, and this should make them deeply suspicious of proposals to engineer the climate that do not carefully seek their fully informed consent.[27] He further suggests that such consent would be unlikely as long as climate engineering is framed in managerial, progress-oriented ways. The only way to talk about climate engineering from an indigenous perspective, he suggests, is to first understand climate change as "an intensification of entangled processes of colonialism, capitalism, and industrialization that continue to inflict harm on indigenous peoples."[28] Once climate change is understood this way, climate engineering becomes a far lower priority than de-colonizing, localizing, and genuinely transformative practices.

In summary, to engineer the climate would be to continue the colonial, progress-obsessed, managerial tendencies that have led to the wicked problems of the 21st century.

Why not engineering the climate might be a bad idea

A consistent ethics of uncertainty, though, must consider the ways we might be wrong. The first way to note this is to once again observe the limits of our voices as authors. As privileged citizens of the industrialized world, we are comfortable saying that people like us should not initiate or advocate for global climate engineering. But if movements for such work came from the grassroots of the two-thirds world or from indigenous communities, we would need to question and likely to pause our own objections in favor of voices that have previously been marginalized and ignored. Should climate engineering be advocated by the marginalized and oppressed, we would quickly reconsider our opposition.

We suspect this would be most possible if proposals to carefully change the climate were moved away from the framework of "engineering" and toward more organic models such as "healing." If the foundational impulse of these technologies was toward helping the climate to restore itself to flourishing, with a focus on the well-being of the planet as an organic whole, these efforts might deserve more serious consideration.[29]

It is also possible that our critiques of climate change are too idealistic, too radical, that we are making the perfect the enemy of the good. Most who advocate for climate engineering would admit at least some of the criticisms we have named above, but would insist that the planetary emergency is such that we simply do not have time for better solutions. De-colonizing practices to heal eco-social systems would be ideal, but perhaps the realistic need is for the best technologies we can come up with which will sustain a livable climate, making it possible to continue if not achieve the struggle for justice. We are not convinced by this kind of pragmatism, but we take it seriously, and we keep open the possibility that we are wrong. Even if we are not wrong, we have much to learn from those with whom we disagree.

This uncertainty is most manifest in our response to proposals to research rather than implement climate engineering. While we would vote and protest strongly against any implementation of solar radiation management or carbon capture and storage, we are less concerned about proposals to continue theoretical analysis of them or even to run small, local tests of these technologies. Some believe that even such research is dangerous, creating false hope and distracting from the real needs of climate mitigation and adaptation.[30] We are too uncertain for such a stance, and we are not resolutely against climate engineering research. Instead, we hope to remain in conversation with such researchers, making our skepticism clear and ensuring that their work is well-monitored and regulated. Uncertainty requires an openness to what more can be known, and there is much more to know about the potential for climate technologies despite our concerns about them.

Ambiguous decisions

Fracking is bad. But not fracking is not perfect. Protesting is good. But not everyone must protest, and we must do much more than protest. Climate engineering is bad. But it raises important questions worthy of continued consideration. There is no ironclad case; every moral absolute can be challenged. Does this leave us stuck in indecision? Faced with ambiguity, what do we do?

Environmentalists should actively oppose fracking, should protest the continued extraction and burning of fossil fuels, and should resist any implementation of climate engineering technologies. However, while taking these stances of resistance, environmentalists must be open and clear about the uncertainty of our own positions and in conversation with those who argue for alternatives. If we can admit that we have no perfect options, then we will be better equipped to carefully choose the best option without blinding ourselves to its imperfections. By accepting that ambiguity of the situation, we become more rather than less able to take decisive action.

To say this a different way, mature environmental ethics must always admit that there will be costs. We can advocate that banning fracking should be accompanied by increased development and deployment of renewable energy technologies, but we cannot be sure it will happen. Banning fracking may lead to more coal being strip-mined and burnt. We can advocate that oil stays in the ground, but we cannot guarantee this as long as oil companies own that oil and have the right to distribute it by other means. We can demand that any new climate technologies be developed in conversation with the poor and marginalized, but we cannot guarantee that this will lead to good outcomes.

Resisting climate change should be part of a broader process of resisting certainty, resisting monological ideas of progress, resisting simplicity. A movement against fracking should seek the kind of humble wonder modeled by

Rachel Carson and Marjory Stoneman Douglas. Protests should be powered by the righteous but pragmatic anger that fueled the struggles of Martin Luther King, Jr., and Malcolm X. All climate engineering proposals should learn from the story of Frank Lloyd Wright about human limitations and the unintended consequences of every decision. This book sought to learn from these figures precisely because they were effective without being perfect, because we believe that a careful study of any one of them can inspire action that accepts ambiguity.

We do not know what moral and environmental decisions might be relevant in your own life, in your community, at the time you are reading this. We hope that you do, or that you will work to find out, and to investigate the stakes, the players, and the complexities of your own situation. We hope that you will embrace the uncertainties of that situation at the pace of ambiguity, critically questioning your own commitments and presuppositions. And we hope that this will empower you to take a stand.

Notes

1 Montgomery & Smith, "Hydraulic Fracturing," 27
2 Lave & Lutz, "Hydraulic Fracturing," 739.
3 Data from the North Dakota Division of Mineral Resources. Accessed Feb. 24, 2019: https://www.dmr.nd.gov/oilgas/stats/historicaloilprodstats.pdf. One barrel of oil equals 42 U.S. gallons, or about 159 liters.
4 Souther, et al., "Biotic Impacts of Energy Development from Shale."
5 Davis & Robinson, "A Geographic Model to Assess and Limit Cumulative Ecological Degradation from Marcellus Shale Exploitation in New York, USA." See also Gleason & Tangen, *Brine Contamination to Aquatic Resources from Oil and Gas Development in the Williston Basin, United States.*
6 Kiviat "Risks to Biodiversity from Hydraulic Fracturing for Natural Gas in the Marcellus and Utica Shales," "especially sodium, chloride, bromide, arsenic, barium, other heavy metals, organic compounds, and radionuclides," p. 3.
7 http://oilprice.com/Energy/Oil-Prices/T.-Boone-Pick
ens-Points-The-Finger-At-U.S-Shale.html
8 Pickens, *First Billion is the Hardest.*
9 Kiviat.
10 Skoumal, et al., "Earthquakes Induced by Hydraulic Fracturing Are Pervasive in Oklahoma," and Schultz, et al., "Hydraulic Fracturing Volume is Associated with Induced Earthquake Productivity in the Duvernay Play."
11 Howarth, et al., "Methane and the Greenhouse-Gas Footprint of Natural Gas from Shale Formations."
12 http://content.sierraclub.org/naturalgas/
13 Associated Press, "Dakota Access Pipeline and a Feeder Line Leaked more than 100 Gallons in March." *The Guardian* May 22, 2017. https://www.theguardian.com/us-news/2017/may/22/dakota-access-pipeline-oil-leak-energy-transfer-partners. Accessed Feb. 11, 2019.
14 Thunberg, Greta. "The Disarming Case to Act Right Now on Climate Change." (2018): Accessed Feb. 11, 2019. https://www.ted.com/talks/greta_thunberg_the_disarming_case_to_act_right_now_on_climate?language=en, and "Speech at UN

Climate Change Cop24 Conference." (2018): Accessed Feb. 11, 2019, https://www.youtube.com/watch?v=VFkQSGyeCWg.

15 "Oceti Sakowin," Stand with Standing Rock. http://standwithstandingrock.net/oceti-sakowin/. Accessed Jan. 15, 2017.

16 "Local Veteran Shares Experiences from Standing Rock" (December 28, 2016), *The Morganton News Herald*, Accessed June 4, 2019,.

17 McKibben, Bill. Twitter Post. Dec. 12, 2018, 10.26 AM. https://twitter.com/billmckibben/status/1072920707007422466.

18 "350 Scientists Back Dutch School Kids Climate Demonstration." Feb. 7 (2019): Accessed Feb. 11, 2019, https://www.dutchnews.nl/news/2019/02/350-scientists-back-dutch-school-kids-climate-demonstration/.

19 Feder, J. Lester, Hirji, Zahra, and Mueller, Pascale. "A Huge Climate Movement Led by Teenage Girls is Sweeping Europe. And it's Coming to the Us Next." Feb. 7 (2019): Accessed Feb. 11, 2019, https://www.buzzfeednews.com/article/lesterfeder/europe-climate-change-protests-teens.

20 "Statement by the President on the Keystone XL Pipeline" (Nov. 5, 2015 Press release), The White House. Accessed January 14, 2017. https://www.whitehouse.gov/the-press-office/2015/11/06/statement-president-keystone-xl-pipeline.

21 "Pipelines Remain Safer Alternative." Accessed Jan. 15, 2017. http://blog.transcanada.com/pipelines-remain-safer-alternative/.

22 Climate engineering is also often referred to as "geoengineering." An introduction to these technologies can be found in British Royal Society, *Geoengineering the Climate*.

23 IPCC, "Summary for Policymakers."

24 Jay Michaelson notes that the U.S. Republican politician Newt Gingrich and the conservative think tank the American Enterprise Institute came out with favorable comments about climate engineering in 2008. It is worth noting that, while suspicious of their politics, Michaelson advises progressive environmentalists to work with such conservatives and to accept the inevitability of climate engineering. (Michaelson, "Geoengineering and Climate Management").

25 The solar radiation management project can be found at https://projects.iq.harvard.edu/keutschgroup/scopex. The private company can be found at http://carbonengineering.com/.

26 Keith, *Case for Climate Engineering*, 173–174.

27 Whyte, "Indigenous Peoples, Solar Radiation Management, and Consent."

28 Whyte, "Indigeneity in Geoengineering Discourses," 9.

29 Laura Hartman suggests that this approach is at least possible and worthy of consideration. See "Healing the Climate? Christian Ethics and Medical Models for Climate Engineering." In Clingerman & O'Brien, *Theological and Ethical Perspectives on Climate Engineering*.

30 See, for example, Hamilton, *Earthmasters*.

REFERENCES

Abram, David. *Becoming Animal: An Earthly Cosmology.* New York: Pantheon Books, 2010.

Abrams, Nancy Ellen. *A God That Could Be Real: Spirituality, Science and the Future of Our Planet.* Boston, MA: Beacon, 2015.

Alexander, Michelle. *The New Jim Crow: Mass Incarceration in the Age of Colorblindness.* New York: New Press, 2010.

Allen, T. F. H., and T. W. Hoekstra. *Toward a Unified Ecology.* New York: Columbia University Press, 1992.

Anderson, Lorriane, and Thomas Edwards, eds. *At Home on This Earth: Two Centuries of US Women's Nature Writing.* Lebanon, NH: University Press of New England, 2002.

Arendt, Hannah. *The Human Condition.* Chicago: University of Chicago Press, 1958.

Arendt, Hannah. *The Promise of Politics.* Jerome Kohn, ed. New York: Schocken Books, 2005.

Avallone, Tommy. Director. *The Bill Murray Stories: Life Lessons Learned from a Mythical Man.* Gravitas Ventures, 2018.

Baldwin, Lewis V. *There is a Balm in Gilead: The Cultural Roots of Martin Luther King, Jr.* Minneapolis: Fortress Press, 1991.

Balslev, Anindita N. *On World Religions: Diversity, Not Dissension.* New Delhi, India: Sage, 2014.

Barad, Karen. *Meeting the Universe Halfway: Quantum Physics and the Entanglement of Matter and Meaning.* Durham, NC: Duke University Press, 2007.

Bauman, Whitney. "South Florida as Matrix for Developing a Planetary Ethic: A Call for Ehtical Per/Versions and Environmental Hospice." *The Journal for Florida Studies* 1, 3 (Spring2014).

Bauman, Whitney. *Religion and Ecology: Developing a Planetary Ethic.* New York: Columbia University Press, 2014.

Bauman, Whitney. "Meaning-Making Practices, Copyrights, and Architecture in the Indonesian Archipelago: Openings toward a Planetary Ethic." *Worldviews: Global Religions, Culture and Ecology* 19, 2 (2015): 184–202.

Bauman, Whitney. "What's Left Out of the Lynn White Narrative." In *Religion and Ecological Crisis: The Lynn White Thesis at 50.* Anna Peterson and Todd LeVasseur, eds. New York: Routledge, 2016, 165–177.

Bauman, Whitney, Richard Bohannon, and Kevin J. O'Brien. *Grounding Religion: A Field Guide to the Study of Religion and Ecology.* 2nd Edition. New York: Routledge, 2017.

Bauman, Whitney, Richard Bohannon, and Kevin J. O'Brien. *Inherited Land: The Changing Grounds of Religion and Ecology*. Eugene, OR: Pickwick Publications, 2011.

Bauman, Zygmunt. *Globalization: The Human Consequences*. Oxford: Blackwell, 1998.

Beavan, Colin. *No Impact Man: The Adventures of a Guilty Liberal Who Attempts to Save the Planet, and the Discoveries He Makes About Himself and Our Way of Life in the Process*. New York: Farrar, Straus and Giroux, 2009.

Bennett, Gaymon. *Technicians of Human Dignity: An Inquiry into the Global Politics of Intrinsic Worth*. New York: Fordham University Press, 2015.

Bennett, Jane. *Vibrant Matter: A Political Ecology of Things*. Durham, NC: Duke University Press, 2010.

Berry, Thomas. *The Great Work: Our Way into the Future*. New York: Bell Tower, 1999.

Berry, Wendell. *A Continuous Harmony: Essays Cultural and Agricultural*. Washington, DC: Shoemaker & Hoard, 1970.

Berry, Wendell. *Citizenship Papers*. Washington, DC: Shoemaker & Hoard, 2003.

Bloch, Ernst. *Principle of Hope*. [3 volumes] Cambridge, MA: MIT Press, 1986.

Boellstorff, Tom. *The Gay Archipelago: Sexuality and Nation in Indonesia*. Princeton: Princeton University Press, 2005.

Boff, Leonardo. *Cry of the Earth, Cry of the Poor*. Maryknoll, NY: Orbis Books, 1997.

Bohannon II, Richard, and Blinnikov, Mikhail. "Habitat Fragmentation and Breeding Bird Population in Western North Dakota after the Introduction of Hydraulic Fracturing." *Annals of the American Association of Geographers*.

Bourdieu, Pierre. *Outline of a Theory of Practice*. Trans. Richard Nice. Cambridge: Cambridge University Press, 1977.

Branch, Michael. "Writing the Swamp: Marjory Stoneman Douglas and The Everglades: River of Grass." In *Such News of the Land: U.S. Women Nature Writers*. Thomas S. Edwards and Elizabeth A. De Wolfe, eds. Hanover, NH: University Press of New England, 2001.

Branch, Taylor. *Pillar of Fire: America in the King Years, 1963–65*. New York, NY: Simon & Schuster, 1998.

Bray, Karen. *Grave Attending: A Political Theology for the Unredeemed*. New York, NY: Fordham University Press, 2019.

Brennan, Teresa. *Globalization and Its Terrors: Daily Life in the West*. New York: Routledge, 2003.

The British Royal Society. *Geoengineering the Climate: Science, Governance, and Uncertainty*. London: Royal Society Reports, 2009.

Brown, Lester R. *Plan B 3.0: Mobilizing to Save Civilization*. New York: Norton, 2008.

Bullard, Robert D., ed. *The Quest for Environmental Justice: Human Rights and the Politics of Pollution*. San Francisco: Sierra Club Books, 2005.

Bullard, Robert D., Mohai, Paul, Saha, Robin, and Wright, Beverly. "Toxic Wastes and Race at Twenty: 1987–2007." (2007): http://www.ucc.org/assets/pdfs/toxic20.pdf (Accessed October 27, 2013).

Burrow, Rufus Jr. *Extremist for Love: Martin Luther King, Jr., Man of Ideas and Nonviolent Social Action*. Minneapolis, MN: Fortress Press, 2014.

Butler, Judith. *Excitable Speech: A Politics of the Performative*. New York, NY: Routledge, 1997.

Campbell, Colin J., and Jean H. Laherrère. "The End of Cheap Oil." *Scientific American* 278, 3 (March1998): 78–83.

Carson, Rachel. *Under the Sea Wind*. New York, NY: Penguin, 1941.

Clark, Kenneth Bancroft. *The Negro Protest: James Baldwin, Malcolm X, Martin Luther King Talk with Kenneth B. Clark.* Boston: Beacon Press, 1963.

Clarke, John Henrik, ed. *Malcolm X: The Man and His Times.* Trenton, NJ: Africa World Press, 1993.

Clingerman, Forrest, and Kevin J. O'Brien. *Theological and Ethical Perspectives on Climate Engineering: Calming the Storm.* Lanham: Lexington Books, 2016.

Cohen, Jeffrey Jerome, ed. *Prismatic Ecology: Ecotheory Beyond Green.* Minneapolis: University of Minnesota Press, 2013.

Cone, James H. *Martin & Malcolm & America: A Dream or a Nightmare.* Maryknoll, NY: Orbis Books, 1991.

Cone, James H. "Whose Earth is it, Anyway?" In *Earth Habitat: Eco-Injustice and the Church's Response.* Dieter T. Hessel and Larry L. Rasmussen, eds. Minneapolis: Fortress Press, 2001.

Connors, Joseph. "Wright on Nature and the Machine." In *The Nature of Frank Lloyd Wright.* Carol R. Bolson, Robert S. Nelson, and Linda Seidel, eds. Chicago: University of Chicago Press, 1988.

Cronon, William. *Uncommon Ground: Rethinking the Human Place in Nature.* New York: Norton, 1995.

Dalke, Anne, and Barbara Dixon, eds. *Minding the Light: Essays in Friendly Pedagogy.* New York: Peter Lang, 2004.

David, Howard Pitney. *Martin Luther King, Jr., Malcolm X, and the Civil Rights Struggle of the 1950s and 1960s: A Brief History with Documents.* Boston: Bedford/St. Martin's, 2004.

Davis, Jack. *An Everglades Providence: Marjory Stoneman Douglas and the American Environmental Century.* Athens, GA: University of Georgia Press, 2009.

Davis, John B., and George R. Robinson. "A Geographic Model to Assess and Limit Cumulative Ecological Degradation from Marcellus Shale Exploitation in New York, USA." *Ecology and Society* 17, 2 (2012).

Deacon, Terrence. *Incomplete Nature: How Mind Emerged from Matter.* New York: WW Norton, 2012.

DeCaro, Louis A. *Malcolm and the Cross: The Nation of Islam, Malcolm X, and Christianity.* New York: New York University Press, 1998.

DeFries, Ruth. *The Big Ratchet: How Humanity Thrives in the Face of Natural Crisis.* New York: Basic Books, 2014.

Deleuze, Gilles, and Felix Guattari. *A Thousand Plateaus: Capitalism and Schizophrenia.* Minneapolis: University of Minnesota Press, 1987.

Derrida, Jacques. *Margins of Philosophy.* Chicago: University of Chicago Press, 1982.

Derrida, Jacques *Spectres of Marx.* New York: Routledge, 1994.

Dillard, Annie. *Pilgrim at Tinker Creek.* New York: HarperCollins, 1974.

Douglas, Marjory Stoneman. *The Everglades: River of Grass.* New York: Rinehart, 1947.

Dyson, Michael Eric. *Open Mike: Reflections on Philosophy, Race, Sex, Culture, and Religion.* New York: Basic Civitas Books, 2002.

Ehrlich, Paul R. *The Population Bomb.* New York: Ballentine Books, 1968.

Ehrlich, Paul R., and Anne H. Ehrlich. *One with Nineveh: Politics, Consumption, and the Human Future.* Washington, DC: Island Press, 2004.

Ehrlich, Paul R. *The Dominant Animal: Human Evolution and the Environment.* Washington, DC: Island Press, 2008.

Ellis, Erle C. *Anthropocene: A Very Short Introduction.* Oxford, UK: Oxford University Press, 2018.

Ellis, Eugenia. "The Red Square: Frank Lloyd Wright, Theosophy, and Modern Conceptions of Space." *Theosophical History* 15, 2 (2011).

Farley, Margaret. *Just Love*. London: Continuum, 2006.

Fishman, Robert. *Urban Utopias in the Twentieth Century: Ebenezer Howard, Frank Lloyd Wright, Le Corbusier*. Cambridge, MA: MIT Press, 1982.

Franklin, Robert Michael Jr. "An Ethic of Hope: The Moral Thought of Martin Luther King, Jr." *Union Seminary Quarterly Review* 40, 4 (1985).

Frederickson, Kari and Jack Davis, eds., *Making Waves: Female Activists in Twentieth-Century Florida*. Gainesville, FL: University Press of Florida, 2003.

Gandhi, Mahatma. *Autobiography: The Story of My Experiments with Truth*. New York: Dover, 1983.

Gebara, Ivone. *Longing for Running Water: Ecofeminism and Liberation*. Minneapolis: Fortress, 1999.

Ghosh, Amitav. *The Great Derangement: Climate Change and the Unthinkable*. Chicago: The University of Chicago Press, 2016.

Gleason, Robert A., and Brian A. Tangen, eds. *Brine Contamination to Aquatic Resources from Oil and Gas Development in the Williston Basin, United States*. Scientific Investigations Report 2014–5017, U.S. Geological Survey, Reston, VA, VA: U.S. Geological Survey 2014. doi:http://dx.doi.org/10.3133/sir20145017 (Accessed November 2014).

Gore, Albert. *An Inconvenient Truth: The Planetary Emergency of Global Warming and What We Can Do About it*. Emmaus, PA: Rodale, 2006.

Gustafson, James M. *Theology and Christian Ethics*. Philadelphia: United Church Press, 1974.

Gustafson, James M. *A Sense of the Divine: The Natural Environment From a Theocentric Perspective*. Cleveland, OH: Pilgrim Press, 1994.

Halberstam, J. Jack (see also Halberstam, Judith). *In a Queer Time and Place: Transgender Bodies, Subcultural Lives*. New York: New York University Press, 2005.

Halberstam, Judith Jack (see also Halberstam, J. Jack). *The Queer Art of Failure*. Durham, NC: Duke University Press, 2011.

Hall, David D. *Lived Religion in America: Toward a History of Practice*. Princeton, NJ: Princeton University Press, 1997.

Hamilton, Clive. *Requiem for a Species: Why We Resist the Truth About Climate Change*. Washington, DC: Earthscan, 2010.

Hamilton, Clive. *Earthmasters: The Dawn of the Age of Climate Engineering*. New Haven, CT: Yale University Press, 2013.

Hansen, James, M. Sato, P. Kharecha, D. Beerling, R. Berner, V. Masson-Delmotte, M. Pagani, M. Raymo, D. L. Royer, and J. C. Zachos. "Target Atmospheric CO_2: Where Should Humanity Aim?" *The Open Atmospheric Science Journal* 2(2008): 217–231.

Hansen, James, P. Kharecha, M. Sato, V. Masson-Delmotte, Frank Ackerman, D. Beerling, Paul J. Hearty, Ove Hoegh-Guldberg, Shi-Ling Hsu, Camille Parmesan, Johan Rockstron, Eelco J. Rohling, Jeffrey Sachs, Pete Smith, Konrad Steffen, Lise Van Susteren, Karina von Schuckmann, and J. C. Zachos. "Assessing 'Dangerous Climate Change': Required Reduction of Carbon Emissions to Protect Young People, Future Generations and Nature." *PLOS One* 8, 12 (2013).

Harding, Vincent. *Martin Luther King, the Inconvenient Hero*. Maryknoll, NY: Orbis Books, 1996.

Harney, Stefano, and Moten, Fred. *The Undercommons: Fugitive Planning and Black Study.* New York: Autonomedia, 2016.

Harris, Melanie L. *Ecowomanism: African American Women and Earth-Honoring Faiths.* Maryknoll: Orbis Books, 2017.

Hawking, Stephen. *Brief Answers to the Big Questions.* New York, NY: Bantam Books, 2018.

Heidegger, Martin. *Question Concerning Technology and Other Essays.* New York: Harper and Row, 1977.

Heise, Ursula K. "From the Blue Planet to Google Earth." *e-Flux* 50 (2013). http://www.e-flux.com/journal/from-the-blue-planet-to-google-earth/ (Accessed April 2016).

Hemmingsen, Emma. "At the Base of Hubbert's Peak: Grounding the Debate on Petroleum Scarcity." *Geoforum* 41 (2010): 531–540.

Hoffman, Donald. "Meeting Nature Face to Face." In *The Nature of Frank Lloyd Wright.* Carol R. Bolson, Robert S. Nelson and Linda Seidel, eds. Chicago: University of Chicago Press. 1988.

Howarth, Robert W., Santoro, Renee, and Ingraffea, Anthony. "Methane and the Greenhouse-gas Footprint of Natural Gas from Shale Formations." *Climate Change* 106, 4 (2011): 679–690.

Hulme, Mike. *Why We Disagree About Climate Change: Understanding Controversy, Inaction and Opportunity.* New York: Cambridge University Press, 2009.

Hyde, Lewis. *Trickster Makes This World: Mischief, Myth, and Art.* New York, NY: Farrar, Straus and Giroux, 1998.

Intergovernmental Panel on Climate Change (IPCC). "Summary for Policymakers." In *Global Warming of 1.5°c. An IPCC Special Report on the Impacts of Global Warming of 1.5°c Above Pre-Industrial Levels and Related Global Greenhouse Gas Emission Pathways, in the Context of Strengthening the Global Response to the Threat of Climate Change, Sustainable Development, and Efforts to Eradicate Poverty.* V. Masson-Delmotte, P. Zhai, H. O. Pörtner, D. Roberts, J. Skea, P. R. Shukla, A. Pirani, W. Moufouma-Okia, C. Péan, R. Pidcock, S. Conners, J. B. R. Matthews, Y. Chen, X. Zhou, M. I. Gomis, E. Lonnoy, T. Maycock, M. Tignor, and T. Waterfield, eds. Geneva, Switzerland: World Meteorological Organization, 2018.

Jenkins, Willis. "After Lynn White: Religious Ethics and Environmental Problems." *Journal of Religious Ethics* 37, 2 (2009): 283–309.

Jenkins, Willis. *The Future of Ethics: Sustainability, Social Justice, and Religious Creativity.* Washington, DC: Georgetown University Press, 2013.

Kearns, Laurel, and Catherine Keller, eds. *Ecospirit: Religions and Philosophies for the Earth.* New York: Fordham University Press, 2007.

Keith, David W. *A Case for Climate Engineering.* Cambridge, MA: MIT Press, 2013.

Keller, Catherine. *Apocalypse Now and Then: A Feminist Guide to the End of the World.* Minneapolis, MN: Fortress, 1996.

Keller, Catherine. *Face of the Deep: A Theology of Becoming.* New York, NY: Routledge, 2003.

Keller, Catherine. *Cloud of the Impossible: Negative Theology and Planetary Entanglement.* New York: Columbia University Press, 2015.

Keller, Catherine. *Political Theology of the Earth: Our Planetary Emergency and the Struggle for a New Public.* New York: Columbia University Press, 2018.

Keller, Catherine, and Laurel Schneider. *Polydoxy: Theology of Multiplicity and Relation.* New York: Routledge, 2011.

King, Martin Luther. *Stride Toward Freedom: The Montgomery Story*. New York: Harper, 1958.

King, Martin Luther. *Why We Can't Wait*. New York: Penguin, 1964.

King, Martin Luther. *Where Do We Go From Here: Chaos or Community?*Boston: Beacon Press, 1967.

King, Martin Luther. *Strength to Love*. Philadelphia: Fortress Press, 1981.

King, Martin Luther. *A Testament of Hope: The Essential Writings of Martin Luther King, Jr.* James M. Washington, ed. San Francisco: HarperCollins, 1986.

Klein, Naomi. *This Changes Everything: Capitalism vs. The Climate*. New York: Simon & Schuster, 2014.

Khan-Cullors, Patrisse, and Asha Bandele. *When They Call You a Terrorist: A Black Lives Matter Memoir*. New York: St. Martin's Press, 2017.

Kim, Grace Ji-Sun, and Hilda P. Koster, eds. *Planetary Solidarity: Global Women's Voices on Christian Doctrine and Climate Justice*. Minneapolis: Fortress Press, 2017.

Kiviat, Erik. "Risks to Biodiversity from Hydraulic Fracturing for Natural Gas in the Marcellus and Utica Shales." *Annals of the New York Academy of Sciences* 1286 (2013): 1–14.

Latour, Bruno. *The Politics of Nature: How to Bring the Sciences into Democracy*. Cambridge, MA: Harvard University Press, 2004.

Latour, Bruno. *Reassembling the Social: An Introduction to Actor-Network Theory*. New York: Oxford University Press, 2005.

Latour, Bruno. "Thou Shalt Not Freeze-Frame or How not to misunderstand the Science and Religion Debate." In *Science, Religion and the Human Experience*. James Proctor, ed. New York: Oxford 2005.

Latour, Bruno. *Facing Gaia: A New Enquiry into Natural Religion*. Edinburgh: University of Edinburgh, 2013.

Latour, Bruno. *Down to Earth: Politics in the New Climatic Regime*. Cambridge, UK; Medford, MA: Polity Press, 2018.

Lave, Rebecca, and Brian Lutz. "Hydraulic Fracturing: A Critical Physical Geography Review." *Geography Compass* 8, 10 (2014): 739–754.

Lee, Hak Joon. *The Great World House: Martin Luther King, Jr., and Global Ethics*. Cleveland: Pilgrim Press, 2011.

Leopold, Aldo. *A Sand County Almanac, with Essays on Conservation from Round River*. New York: Ballantine Books, 1966.

Lewis, Hope. "Race, Class, and Katrina: Human Rights and (Un)Natural Disaster." In *Environmental Justice in the New Millenium: Global Perspectives on Race, Ethnicity, and Human Rights*. Filomina Chioma Steady, ed. London: Palgrave Macmillan, 2009.

Light, Andrew. "The Urban Blind Spot in Environmental Ethics." *Environmental Politics* 10, 1 (2001): 7–25.

Lomborg, Bjørn. *The Skeptical Environmentalist: Measuring the Real State of the World*. New York: Cambridge University Press, 2001.

Lomborg, Bjørn. *Cool It: The Skeptical Environmentalist's Guide to Global Warming*. New York: Vintage Books, 2008.

Lytle, Mark H. *The Gentle Subversive: Rachel Carson, Silent Spring, and the Rise of the Environmental Movement*. New York: Oxford, 2007.

McFague, Sallie. *Life Abundant: Rethinking Theology and Economy for a Planet in Peril*. Minneapolis, MN: Fortress Press, 2001.

McFague, Sallie. *A New Climate for Theology: God, the World, and Global Warming.* Minneapolis, MN: Fortress Press, 2008.

McNeill, John Robert, and Peter Engelke. *The Great Acceleration: An Environmental History of the Anthropocene Since 1945.* Cambridge, MA: The Belknap Press of Harvard University Press, 2016.

Menocal, Narciso G. "The Sources of Frank Lloyd Wright's Architectural Utopia: Variations on a Theme of Nature." In *Utopian Vision, Technological Innovation, and Poetic Imagination.* Klaus L. Berghahn and Reinhold Grimm, eds. Heidelberg: Winter, 1990.

Merchant, Carolyn. *Reinventing Eden: The Fate of Nature in Western Culture.* New York, NY: Routledge, 2003.

Michaelson, Jay. "Geoengineering and Climate Management: From Marginality to Inevitability." In *Climate Change Geoengineering: Philosophical Perspectives, Legal Issues, and Governance Frameworks.* Wil C. G. Burns and Andrew L. Strauss, eds. New York: Cambridge University Press, 2013: 81–114.

Moe-Lobeda, Cynthia D. *Resisting Structural Evil: Love as Ecological-Economic Vocation.* Minneapolis, MN: Fortress Press, 2013.

Montgomery, Carl T., and Michael B. Smith. "Hydraulic Fracturing: History of an Enduring Technology." *Journal of Petroleum Technology* 12 (2010): 26–32.

Moore, Jason W., ed. *Anthropocene or Capitalocene? Nature, History, and the Crisis of Capitalism.* Oakland, CA: PM Press, 2016.

Mortimer-Sandilands, Catriona, and Bruce Erickson, eds. *Queer Ecologies: Sex, Nature, Politics and Desire.* Bloomington: Indiana University Press, 2010.

Morton, Nelle. *The Journey is Home.* Boston, MA: Beacon, 1985.

Morton, Timothy. *Hyperobjects: Philosophy and Ecology after the End of the World.* Minneapolis: University of Minnesota Press, 2013.

Muir, John. *My First Summer in the Sierra.* San Francisco: Sierra Club Books, 1988.

Nixon, Rob. *Slow Violence and the Environmentalism of the Poor.* Cambridge, MA: Harvard University Press, 2011.

Northcott, Michael S. *The Environment and Christian Ethics.* New York: Cambridge University Press, 1996.

Northcott, Michael S. *A Moral Climate: The Ethics of Global Warming.* Maryknoll, NY: Orbis Books, 2007.

Northcott, Michael S. "The Concealment of Carbon Markets and the Publicity of Love in a Time of Climate Change." *International Journal of Public Theology* 4 (2010): 294–313.

O'Brien, Kevin J. "The 'War' Against Climate Change and Christian Eco-Justice: Ethical Implications of Martial Rhetoric." *Worldviews* 16 (2012): 135–153

O'Brien, Kevin J. *The Violence of Climate Change: Lessons of Resistance from Nonviolent Activists.* Washington, DC: Georgetown University Press, 2017.

Ogle, Vanessa. *The Global Transformation of Time 1870–1950.* Cambridge, MA: Harvard University Press, 2015.

Pellow, David N. "Toward a Critical Environmental Justice Studies: Black Lives Matter as an Environmental Justice Challenge." *Du Bois Review* 13, 2 (2016): 221–236.

Peterson, Anna Lisa. *Seeds of the Kingdom: Utopian Communities in the Americas.* New York: Oxford, 2005.

Peterson, Anna Lisa. *Everyday Ethics and Social Change: The Education of Desire.* New York: Columbia University Press, 2009.

Pickens, T. Boone. *The First Billion is the Hardest: How Believing it's Still Early in the Game Can Lead to Life's Greatest Comebacks.* New York: Crown Publishers, 2008.

Plumwood, Val. *Environmental Culture: The Ecological Crisis of Reason.* New York, NY: Routledge, 2002.

Pope Francis. *Laudato Si': On Care for Our Common Home.* Vatican City: Encyclical Letter, 2015.

Rabaka, Reiland. "Malcolm X and/as Critical Theory: Philosophy, Radical Politics, and the African American Search for Social Justice." *Journal of Black Studies* 33 (2002).

Riley, Matthew. "The Democratic Roots of our Ecologic Crisis: Lynn White, Bio-democracy, and the Earth Charter." *Zygon: Journal of Religion and Science* 49, 4 (December2014): 938–948.

Rittel, Horst W.J., and Melvin Webber. "Dilemmas in a General Theory of Planning." *Policy Sciences* 4(1973).

Rubenstein, Mary Jane. *Worlds without End: The Many Lives of the Multiverse.* New York: Columbia University Press, 2014.

Ruether, Rosemary Radford. *Integrating Ecofeminism, Globalization, and World Religions.* Lanham, MD: Rowman & Littlefield, 2004.

Sabin, Paul. *The Bet: Paul Ehrlich, Julian Simon, and Our Gamble over Earth's Future.* New Haven, CT: Yale University Press, 2013.

Savoy, Lauret E. *Trace: Memory, History, Race, and the American Landscape.* Berkeley, California: Counterpoint, 2015.

Schultz, R., Atkinson, G., Eaton, D. W., Gu, Y. J., and Kao, H. "Hydraulic Fracturing Volume is Associated with Induced Earthquake Productivity in the Duvernay Play." *Science* 359, 6737 (January2018): 304–308.

Schweitzer, Albert. *On the Edge of the Primeval Forest.* New York: Macmillan, 1931.

Schweitzer, Albert, and Lilian M. Russell. *Indian Thought and Its Development.* London: Hodder and Stoughton, 1936.

Shotwell, Alexis. *Against Purity: Living Ethically in Compromised Times.* Minneapolis: University of Minnesota Press, 2016.

Sideris, Lisa H. "On Letting a Thousand Flowers Bloom: Religious Scholarship in a Time of Crisis." *Journal of the American Academy of Religion* 83, 2 (2015).

Sideris, Lisa H. "Science as Sacred Myth? Ecospirituality in the Anthropocene Age." *Journal for the Study of Religion, Nature, and Culture* 9, 2 (2015): 136–153.

Sideris, Lisa H. *Consecrating Science: Wonder, Knowledge, and the Natural World.* Oakland: University of California Press, 2017.

Sideris, Lisa and Kathleen Dean Moore, eds. *Rachel Carson, Legacy and Challenge.* Albany, NY: Statue University of New York Press, 2008.

Sieden, Lloyd Steven. *Buckminster Fuller's Universe: His Life and Work.* New York: Basic Books, 1989.

Sitkoff, Harvard. *King: Pilgrimage to the Mountaintop.* New York: Hill and Wang, 2008.

Skoumal, Robert J., Ries, Rosmiel, Brudzinski, Michael R., Barbour, Andrew J., Currie, and Brian S. "Earthquakes Induced by Hydraulic Fracturing Are Pervasive in Oklahoma." *Journal of Geophysical Research: Solid Earth* 123, 12 (November, 2018)

Smith, Kathryn. 2005. "A Beat of the Rhythmic Clock of Nature: Wright's Waterfall Buildings." In *On and By Frank Lloyd Wright: A Primer of Architectural Principles.* Robert McCarter, ed. London: Phaidon, 2005.

Snyder, Gary. *The Practice of the Wild: Essays.* San Francisco: North Point Press, 1990.

Soleri, Paolo. *The Omega Seed: An Eschatological Hypothesis.* Garden City, NY: Anchor Books, 1981.

Souder, William. *On a Farther Shore: The Life and Legacy of Rachel Carson*. New York: Broadway Books, 2012.

Steingraber, Sandra. *Living Downstream: An Ecologist Looks at Cancer and the Environment*. Reading, MA: Addison-Wesley, 1997.

Souther, Sara, Morgan W. Tingley, Viorel D. Popescu, David T. S. Hayman, Maureen E. Ryan, Tabitha A. Graves, Brett Hartl, and Kimberly Terrell. 2014. "Biotic Impacts of Energy Development from Shale: Research Priorities and Knowledge Gaps." *Frontiers in Ecology and the Environment* 12, 6 (2014): 330–338.

Stengers, Isabel. "The Cosmopolitical Proposal." In *Making Things Public*. Bruno Latour and Peter Weibel, eds. Cambridge, MA: The MIT Press, 2005.

Stengers, Isabel. *Cosmopolitics I*. Minneapolis, MN: University of Minnesota Press, 2010.

Stenmark, Lisa. "An Ecology of Knowledge: Feminism, Ecology and the Science and Religion Discourse." *Metaviews: The Listserv of the Metanexus Institute* (February 5, 2011): http://cstl-csm.semo.edu/agathman/ui415/An%20Ecology%20of%20Knowledge.htm)Accessed March 28, 2019).

Stenmark, Lisa. "Developing an Apocalyptic Vision: Postcolonial and Indigenous Science Fiction and Hope for a New World." *American Academy of Religion Meeting* (Atlanta, GA: November 22, 2015).

Swimme, Brian, and Thomas Berry. *The Universe Story: From the Primordial Flaring Forth to the Ecozoic Era—A Celebration of the Unfolding of the Cosmos*. San Francisco: HarperSan Francisco, 1992.

Tal, Alon. *Speaking of Earth: Environmental Speeches That Moved the World*. New Brunswick, NJ: Rutgers University Press, 2006.

Taylor, Astra, Bill Imperial, Lea Marin, John M. Tran, Robert Kennedy, Cornel West, Avital Ronell, et al. 2010. *Examined Life*. [Montréal]: National Film Board of Canada.

Terrill, Robert E. "Protest, Prophecy, and Prudence in the Rhetoric of Malcolm X." *Rhetoric & Public Affairs* 4, 1 (2001).

Terrill, Robert E. "Judgment and Critique in the Rhetoric of Malcolm X." In *The Cambridge Companion to Malcolm X*. New York: Cambridge University Press, 2010.

Thoreau, Henry D. *Walden*. Cambridge, MA: Thomas Y. Crowell & Company, 1910.

Tillich, Paul. *Dynamics of Faith*. New York: Harper & Row, 1957

Trible, Phyllis. *Texts of Terror: Literary-Feminist Readings of Biblical Narratives*. Philadelphia: Fortress Press, 1984.

Tyner, James A. *The Geography of Malcolm X: Black Radicalism and the Remaking of American Space*. New York: Routledge, 2006.

Uechi, Naomi Tanabe. "Evolving Transcendentalism: Thoreauvian Simplicity in Frank Lloyd Wright's Taliesin and Contemporary Ecological Architecture." *The Concord Saunterer* 17 (2009), 73–98.

Uechi, Naomi Tanabe, *Evolving Transcendentalism in Literature and Architecture: Frank Furness, Louis Sullivan, and Frank Lloyd Wright*. Newcastle upon Tyne: Cambridge Scholars Publishing, 2013.

U.S. Geological Survey. "Assessment of Undiscovered Oil Resources in the Bakken and Three Forks Formations, Williston Basin Province, Montana, North Dakota, and South Dakota, 2013." Fact Sheet 2013–3013, U.S. Department of the Interior, 2013.

Vitek, William, and Wes Jackson. *The Virtues of Ignorance: Complexity, Sustainability, and the Limits of Knowledge*. Lexington, KY: University Press of Kentucky, 2008.

Vogel, Steven. *Thinking Like a Mall: Environmental Philosophy After the End of Nature*. Cambridge, MA: MIT Press, 2015.

Wapner, Paul Kevin. *Living Through the End of Nature: The Future of American Environmentalism*. Cambridge, MA: MIT Press, 2010.

Watson, Joseph M. "The Suburbanity of Frank Lloyd Wright's Broadacre City." *Journal of Urban History* (November2018).

White Jr, Lynn. "The Historical Roots of Our Ecologic Crisis." *Science* 155, 3767 (1967).

Whitehead, Alfred North. *Science and the Modern World*. New York: MacMillan, 1925.

Whyte, Kyle Powys. "Indigenous Peoples, Solar Radiation Management, and Consent." In *Engineering the Climate: The Ethics of Solar Radiation Management*. Christopher J. Preston, ed. Lanham, MA: Lexington Books, 2012, 65–76.

Whyte, Kyle Powys. "Is it Colonial Déja Vu? Indigenous Peoples and Climate Injustice." In *Humanities for the Environment: Integrating Knowledges, Forging New Constellations of Practice*. Joni Adamson, Michael Davis, and Hsinya Huang, eds. London: Earthscan, 2016, 88–104.

Whyte, Kyle Powys. "Indigeneity in Geoengineering Discourses: Some Considerations." *Ethics, Policy & Environment* 21, 3 (January2019): 289–307.

Wilson, Edward O. *Biophilia*. Cambridge, MA: Harvard University Press, 1984.

Wilson, Edward O. *Naturalist*. Washington, DC: Island Press, 1994.

Wilson, Edward O. *Consilience: The Unity of Knowledge*. New York: Knopf, 1998.

Wilson, Edward O. *The Future of Life*. New York: Vintage, 2002.

Wilson, Edward O. *The Meaning of Human Existence*. New York: Norton, 2014.

Wright, Frank Lloyd. *An Autobiography*. New York: Horizon Press, 1932.

Yusoff, Kathryn. *A Billion Black Anthropocenes or None*. Minneapolis: University of Minnesota Press, 2018.

X, Malcolm and Alex Haley. *The Autobiography of Malcolm X*. New York: Grove Press, 1965.

X, Malcolm and George Breitman. *Malcolm X Speaks: Selected Speeches and Statements*. New York: Grove Press, 1965.

X, Malcolm and George Breitman. *By Any Means Necessary: Speeches, Interviews, and a Letter*. New York: Pathfinder Press, 1970.

X, Malcolm and Bruce Perry. *Malcolm X: The Last Speeches*. New York: Pathfinder, 1989.

Zachariah, George. *Alternatives Unincorporated: Earth Ethics From the Grassroots*. London: Equinox, 2011.

INDEX

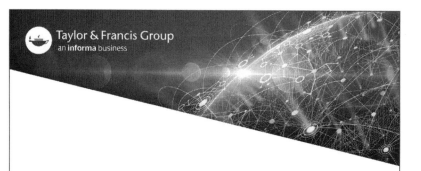

Printed in Great Britain
by Amazon

68541010R00093